Student-Led Devotions for Youth Ministry

Group

Loveland, Colorado

Student-Led Devotions for Youth Ministry

Thanks to the authors and editors of Group's Active Bible Curriculum® from which this book was compiled.

Credits
Editors: Stephen Parolini and Helen Turnbull
Book Acquisitions Editor: Amy Simpson
Creative Development Editor: Dave Thornton
Chief Creative Officer: Joani Schultz
Copy Editor: Janis Sampson
Designer and Art Director: Jean Bruns
Cover Art Director: Jeff A. Storm
Computer Graphic Artist: Joyce Douglas
Cover Designer: Diana Walters
Cover Photography: FPG Stock Photography
Production Manager: Gingar Kunkel

Library of Congress Cataloging-in-Publication Data
Student-led devotions for youth ministry.
        p.   cm.
     ISBN 0-7644-2004-6
     1. Church group work with teenagers.
BV4447.S728 1998
259' .23–dc21
                                    97-52301
                                       CIP

10 9 8 7 6 5 4 3   07 06 05 04 03 02 01 00

Printed in the United States of America.

Visit our Web site: www.grouppublishing.com

Contents

Introduction

Ever wonder how to bridge the generation gap with your kids? Do they lose interest during meetings or miss the point of your activities? Ever wonder if *you* really got the point of a lesson or activity? Then maybe it's time to let someone else lead!

This collection of thirty-eight student-led devotions is designed to help teenagers to get the point by immersing them in experiences that help bring the point to life. Like many Group books, *Student-Led Devotions for Youth Ministry* uses active learning to help the group members understand and apply the message of the activity.

Active learning leads students in doing things that help them understand important principles, messages, and ideas. It's a discovery process that helps kids internalize what they learn. Active learning means learning by doing. And there's no better way for your kids to learn about responsibility, decision-making, and leadership than by leading devotions themselves.

Each activity in this book includes an experience designed to evoke specific feelings in the students. The activities also process those feelings through "How did you feel?" or "What was that like?" questions and apply the message to situations that kids face.

Dive into the activities with your group members. Don't be a spectator; be sure to participate as one of the students. Make sure you plan ahead with your student-leader so he or she will have plenty of time to prepare. And be prepared to answer questions your student-leader may have ahead of time. You may want to photocopy the "Tips for Leading Devotions" handout (p. 6) for your student-leaders, to give them some ideas on how to use these devotions.

And be sure to check out the Scripture and Topical Indexes (p. 127) for a quick survey of what's included in these learning experiences.

If you're looking for activities that you and your kids will remember, look no further: *Student-Led Devotions for Youth Ministry* is your resource.

Tips for Leading Devotions

Plan Ahead

Preparation is essential in making your devotion run smoothly. Be sure you do all these things before you lead your devotion:

- Carefully read through the devotion ahead of time.
- Work with your youth leader to determine how much time you'll need and how much time you're allotted. Practice your devotion so you can be sure to stay on schedule.
- Be sure you have all the supplies needed for the lesson.
- Use a bookmark for the Scriptures you'll use so you can refer to them quickly when necessary.
- Anticipate where you'll need extra help, and designate volunteers before you begin.
- Determine how many students you'll have for your devotion, and adjust the activities accordingly.

Personalize the Devotion

You don't have to read the devotion word for word unless you're more comfortable doing that. If you feel the need to change an activity slightly to suit your needs, be sure to check with your youth group leader to make sure your changes are appropriate.

Pick a devotion you're interested in, and read up on the subject. You also might want to gather magazine articles, books, or music that's relevant to your subject and incorporate them into your devotion.

Follow Up With Discussion

An important part of leading a devotion is asking thought-provoking questions. Always make sure you have time for the discussion questions that follow an activity. Encourage everyone to participate, but don't force students to respond if they seem uncomfortable.

Sometimes you may only need to ask one question to have a good discussion. At other times, you may have to ask a lot of questions and prompt answers. In these cases, use the possible responses that follow each question to help generate a good discussion.

Alien Detection

Purpose:
Teenagers will explore how to live as citizens of heaven while still on earth.

Supplies:
You'll need Bibles, newsprint, markers, tape, a pencil, and paper.

Experience:

Before the meeting, ask three or four people to act as "aliens" in this section of the lesson. Tell them to answer other students' questions honestly and not to act strangely. Here are some suggestions for producing subtle alien characteristics:

- change the color of their tongues using food coloring,
- put fake moles on their ear lobes using a black watercolor marker, or
- have all aliens stand on one foot while talking.

Feel free to use your own ideas for distinguishing your aliens.

Say: **Before we look at how we can live as citizens of heaven on earth, let's see what we might look like to those who don't know Jesus.**

There are aliens among us! I know because they each have unique characteristics that set them apart. Your job is to mingle and talk until you can uncover who among us are from another planet. Go!

After the aliens have been discovered, call everyone together and ask:

- **What was it like being an alien?** *(I knew I was different; I didn't want people to notice what was different about me.)*

- **Are these feelings like feelings we sometimes have as Christians in a non-Christian world? How?** *(Sometimes I don't want people to know I'm a Christian; it's hard being different.)*

- **What are the distinguishing characteristics that a citizen of heaven on earth might have?** *(She would show love; he would worship God.)*

Say: **Heaven is a real place, and all Christians will live there someday. But even while we're here, we're still citizens of heaven. And that means we need to live lives that help others see where we're going.**

Form two groups, and give each group a Bible. Assign each group one of these passages: Matthew 6:9-13 and 1 John 3:2-3. Have groups read their passages and decide how the passages apply to living as citizens of heaven now.

Say to the Matthew 6:9-13 group: **Your job is to create a list of ways we can accomplish God's will on earth in our daily lives. Write the list on newsprint, and tape it to the wall. You might list things such as feeding the hungry, stopping war, loving your neighbor, or obeying your parents.** Give this group a sheet of newsprint, a marker, and tape.

Say to the 1 John 3:2-3 group: **Your job is to create a poem about your own lives based on the passage. It doesn't have to rhyme or even sound poetic. It just has to explain how the passage relates to the way you live. Title it "Now and Not Yet."** Give this group a sheet of paper and a pencil.

Give groups their supplies, and allow them to work for several minutes. Then have them each read their project to the other group.

Ask:

● **Based on what we've seen here, how do Christians live on earth as citizens of heaven?** *(By living according to God's commands; by keeping our eyes focused on Jesus.)*

● **What can you do today to live as a citizen of heaven?** *(Pray more; tell others about my faith; follow Christ's example.)*

Say: **God's gift of eternal life is free. But when we accept it, we need to commit ourselves to serving him because of what he's done for us. And that commitment starts by choosing to live as citizens of heaven while we're still here on earth.**

Alone With God

Purpose:

Teenagers will learn that God is always near and ready to hear their prayers.

Supplies:

None

Experience:

For this activity, you'll need to be able to make the room as dark as possible. If necessary, tape black plastic over windows to shut out light that enters the room. Or meet in a room that's easily darkened.

Begin this activity with students in a circle and the lights on. Have volunteers pray, asking God to help the class learn more about the power of prayer. If students haven't prayed much before, say that prayer is simply communicating with God. You may want to give them an example of a simple prayer. After a minute or so of praying, form two groups and separate them in the room. Have groups each continue to pray about any topics they like. After another minute, divide the two groups into four groups and separate them in the room. Continue to shrink the size of the groups until each person is sitting by him- or herself in the room. Then turn out the lights.

Say: **In silence, continue your prayers. But now it's just you and God. Take the next three minutes to talk with God silently—and let him talk to you.**

Students will probably get uncomfortable about praying for three minutes in silence. That's OK. You'll discuss their feelings when time is up.

After three minutes (with the lights still off and kids still by themselves), ask:

● **What's it like to be alone with God?** *(I felt uncomfortable; it was strange; I felt at peace; I didn't feel God's presence.)*

● **How do the prayer times with other group members compare to your quiet time alone?** *(I like the group prayers better; I feel more comfortable with God alone.)*

● **What do your feelings when you're alone with God say about your relationship with God?** *(If you're uncomfortable alone with God, you might need to work on your relationship with him; if you feel good when alone with God, your relationship is probably good.)*

● **Why is time alone with God important?** *(Because it refreshes us;*

because it helps us grow in faith; because it's when we communicate best with God.)

Say: **Before Jesus was crucified, he went to a place called Gethsemane with his disciples. But his disciples couldn't stay awake while Jesus prayed because they were tired. Unlike Jesus, the disciples didn't fully comprehend the importance of prayer in this time of great trial. Yet this time Jesus spent alone with God paints a vivid picture of the importance and power of prayer.**

Have volunteers act out Matthew 26:36-46. You'll need a person to play the role of Jesus and others to play the roles of the disciples. Read the story aloud as students act it out.

Ask:

● **How do you think Jesus felt in this situation?** *(Frustrated; upset; anxious.)*

● **Why did Jesus want his disciples to stay awake with him?** *(He wanted company; he was overwhelmed with sadness and wanted their support.)*

● **How is Jesus' time alone with God like the time you spent alone with God in the previous activity?** *(God was listening to each prayer; Jesus was in a crisis situation, we weren't; time alone with God is energizing.)*

● **What did Jesus gain from his prayer time with God?** *(Strength to keep going; confidence; comfort; a challenge to move forward.)*

● **What can we gain from our prayer times with God?** *(Strength; confidence; comfort.)*

● **What benefits does prayer have for you?** *(It gives me answers to problems; it makes me feel close to God; it strengthens my faith.)*

Form groups of no more than five. Give each group a Bible. Say: **Have members in your group take turns reading aloud the verses of Psalm 69. After reading the psalm, talk about how it made you feel. Then, one at a time, describe a time you felt lost or abandoned and how you were able to get beyond your feeling of loneliness.**

After students finish sharing their stories, say: **You may feel frustrated or scared—just as Jesus was—as you face trials in your life. But God is always near—you can reach out to him in prayer, no matter what situation you're in.**

Angels and Obstacles

Purpose:

Teenagers will explore how God uses angels to help guide people.

Supplies:

You'll need two large marshmallows and a one-foot length of masking tape for every two students, paper, and pencils.

Experience:

Have a few volunteers create an obstacle course using things around the room, such as chairs, tables, books, or pieces of paper. Form pairs, and give each pair two large marshmallows and a strip of masking tape approximately a foot long. Have everyone stand on the opposite side of the room from where you are.

Say: **In your pairs, designate one person to be an "angel" and one person to be a "walker."**

Give kids ten seconds to assign roles.

Say: **If you're the angel, blindfold your partner by lightly taping the marshmallows over his or her eyes, being careful not to get tape in your partner's hair.**

Give pairs a minute to do this, then have all the angels and walkers face you and line up against the wall opposite you.

Say: **Walkers, your goal is to walk to me without touching any obstacle. As you're walking, I'll give you specific instructions such as "Stop" or "Turn around." If you don't follow my instructions exactly, or if you hit any obstacle while you're walking, you'll have to go back to the beginning.**

Angels, your job is to make sure your partners don't hit any obstacles. You can't speak to your partners or touch them, but you may use yourselves to block your partners from obstacles. The first pair to reach me wins. Go!

As students are walking, call out the following instructions, adding some of your own:

Stop! Turn around three times before continuing.

Stop! Face the opposite direction and take three steps.

Hop on one foot for the next ten seconds.

Stop walking and crawl on your hands and knees until I tell you otherwise.

Look for any pairs who hit obstacles, and make them go back to the beginning. When a team finally reaches you, allow the walker to remove the marshmallow blindfold. Award winners the remaining marshmallows.

Ask:

● **If you were a walker, how did it feel to walk without being able to see? Explain.** *(Scary, I thought I'd hit something; confusing, I didn't know where to put my foot next.)*

● **If you were an angel, how did it feel to protect your partner from hitting obstacles? Explain.** *(Frustrating, I didn't know where he or she was going to go next; exciting, I had to be alert.)*

● **If you were a walker, what difference did it make knowing there was an angel there to help you? Explain.** *(Not much, I can't trust someone I can't talk to or see; a lot, I knew she wouldn't let me hit an obstacle.)*

● **Do you think there really are angels around us helping us? Explain.** *(Yes, the Bible talks about angels; no, if angels were helping me, I wouldn't get in so much trouble.)*

● **The Bible says one role of angels is to guide us. If angels are around us, how might their actions be like the actions of the angels in this activity?** *(We can't always see dangers, and angels could move us away from them; we don't always see the help we might be getting from angels; I'm always bumping into stuff.)*

Say: **We don't always see what goes on behind the scenes. God may have angels helping us when we're unaware we need help. Let's explore the Bible to find specific ways God has used angels to help people in the past.**

Form five groups of about equal sizes. (A group can be one person if necessary.) Each group will need at least one Bible.

Say: **There are nearly three hundred references to angels in the Bible. Let's look at a few to see what angels do and determine if they're still around today.**

Assign each group one of the following sets of passages:

Group 1: Genesis 24:40; Exodus 23:20; and 1 Kings 19:1-8.

Group 2: Judges 6:11-23; Judges 13:6-7; and Luke 2:8-15.

Group 3: 2 Samuel 24:15-16; 2 Kings 19:32-36; and 1 Chronicles 21:30.

Group 4: Matthew 13:49; Matthew 25:31; and 2 Thessalonians 1:7.

Group 5: Luke 15:10; Hebrews 1:14; and Hebrews 13:2.

Have each group read its passages together, determining what angels do according to the verses.

After five minutes, have each person find two new partners from other groups. Provide each group with pencil and paper. Have each group select one person as a representative who will act as a spokesperson, another as a recorder, and the third as an encourager who will ensure everyone in the group has shared.

Say: **Share with your group what you discovered in your previous group. Together come up with a larger definition of what angels do; then try to determine if they're still active today based on the information you've gathered.**

Allow five minutes for discussion, then ask:

● **What are some of the roles angels have played in the past?** *(Guide; God's messenger; protector.)*

● **How did people who encountered these angels feel about them?** *(Afraid; they didn't even know they were angels at first, but when they found out, they were scared; glad for the angel's help.)*

● **How do you think you'd feel if you met an angel? Explain.** *(Afraid, because they're so powerful; special since God was giving me a private message; safe from harm.)*

● **From what you've read today, do you think angels are still around? Explain.** *(Yes, because the Bible tells of their role in future events such as the end of the world; yes, because the Bible says we might not know if someone around us is an angel; no, because in the Bible angels usually identified themselves, and no one's ever come up to me and said he was an angel.)*

● **Has there ever been a time when you felt like you were being helped by an angel? Explain.** *(Allow students to respond.)*

Say: **God knows what the world is like and that we need his help. God's angels, as powerful and obedient servants, helped many people in history by following God's directions. It's possible they're still helping us at God's command. Wouldn't it be great if we reacted the same way to God's commands?**

Attack of the Killer Marshmallows

Purpose:

Teenagers will learn that we need to rely on God constantly for his protection and not go our own way.

Supplies:

You'll need newspapers, masking tape, marshmallows, markers, poster board, and scissors. Ahead of time, gather together a box full of old clothes such as shirts, pants, shoes, and hats.

Experience:

Form groups of four or five. Station the groups around the room, apart from each other. Have the person in each group whose birthday is closest to today become the "protected one." Give groups a lot of newspapers and masking tape and tell them to use the papers and tape to shield their protected one from an attack of marshmallows. Tell them that no part of the body should be vulnerable to a marshmallow attack. Students will want to cover their protected one with the newspaper (like a scuba suit).

Give students about five minutes to make a shelter or armor to protect their protected one. When all groups are ready, say: **I'm going to give each person, except for the protected ones, one marshmallow. You are to try to "wound" another team's protected one by hitting him or her with a marshmallow on the skin or clothing. You must stay at least six feet away from a person to throw your marshmallow, and you may throw it only once.**

Hand out the marshmallows, and give kids the "go" signal. Be sure to stop the action quickly after each person has thrown his or her marshmallow. Go around and judge the "safety" of each group's protected one, based on the amount of clothing or skin that isn't covered. Then have students unwrap the protected ones and all join together.

Ask:

● **Protected ones, what did it feel like to be under attack?** *(Weird, I couldn't even see; fun, I knew I was safe.)*

● **How effectively did your group protect you?** *(Great, no marks; not so good.)*

● **Was there one way your group protected you that was better than another? Why or why not?** *(Yes, ours was best because it worked; no, some kids just got lucky.)*

● **How was this experience like the way God protects us from spiritual attacks?** *(His protection is a lot better; he saves us from a lot worse things than marshmallows.)*

Say: **How well we're protected depends on our armor. Let's see how well God's protection will armor us.**

Have students turn to Ephesians 6:10-13. Ask a volunteer to read the passage aloud.

Then say: **The rest of this passage is probably familiar to you. But today we're going to take a little different look at it. We're going to compare the armor listed here to a firefighter's armor.**

Form three groups. A group can be one person. Assign each group one of the following passages: Ephesians 6:14; 6:15-16; and 6:17. Bring out the box of old clothes and the markers, poster board, and scissors.

Say: **Read through your verse or verses and create from these materials a piece of firefighter's equipment that compares to the spiritual armor in your passage. Be sure to write on the equipment the name of the armor it represents.**

Give groups about five minutes to create their firefighter's equipment. Then select one volunteer to model all the equipment. He or she should leave it on for the rest of this activity. Have groups explain the pieces they created.

Then ask:

● **How does each piece of spiritual armor help us?**

Go through each piece listed in the passage, having students suggest ways the piece of armor helps them in real life. Encourage kids to be specific.

When you've finished with verses 14 through 17, read aloud Ephesians 6:18.

Ask:

● **How does this added element of protection help us?** *(It gives us contact with the One who can help us; it's like a firefighter's water hose.)*

Say: **With all this protection, we ought to be in pretty good shape! But sometimes we set out on our own without all the protection. And then we get into trouble. We need to learn to constantly lean on God for his protection and not go our own way.**

Beyond the
World We Know

Purpose:

Teenagers will explore why heaven is a reality God expects us to take seriously.

Supplies:

You'll need Bibles, paper, tape, newspapers, pencils, and a copy of the "Dream Vacation" handout (p. 18) for each person.

Experience:

Give each person a sheet of paper, and have them each tear the paper to represent something they value in this world. For example, a student could make a representation of a car or a friendship. When students are ready, have them explain what they created.

Form groups of six or fewer, and give each group tape and a stack of newspapers. Say: **Using the newspapers and tape, create a "cocoon" in which your entire group will be completely hidden from my sight. You can use any other props you can find in this room.**

Give groups several minutes to create their cocoons. Make sure kids are completely concealed in their newspaper cocoons, and instruct them to take their torn-paper creations inside with them. When groups are all "cocooned," ask:

● **What's it like to be sealed off from the rest of the room?** *(It's fun to hide; it feels a little stuffy.)*

Say: **Let's say your little cocoon is like life on earth. You have all your friends here, and all the things you value. But there's a whole lot more in this room than what you can see.**

Ask:

● **Is this like the difference between earth and heaven? How?** *(We can only see and understand a little of the whole picture while we're alive on earth; in heaven, we'll understand everything about life.)*

● **From this experience, why is it hard for us to understand what**

life in heaven must be like? *(We can only see our limited experiences; heaven could be totally different from life on earth, and we can't see it to know what it's like.)*

● **How does this experience make you feel about heaven? Explain.** *(Curious, because I wonder how it will be different from life on earth; excited, because I want to see what it's like where God lives.)*

Say: **It really is hard to understand what heaven is like. Our limited human language falls short because we don't have the words to describe heaven. Fortunately, God has not left us completely in the dark. We have his Word to help us understand the reality of heaven, even though it's totally different from life here on earth.**

Have group members tear their way out of their cocoons, and give each person the "Dream Vacation" handout (p. 18), a Bible, and a pencil. Have someone read aloud Revelation 21:1-7, 15-27. Then say: **Suppose you had the chance to check out heaven before you die. What would you like to see on this unusual vacation?**

Have students complete their handouts by following the instructions written there. When they're finished, have them form groups of four, and take turns telling their group members what their favorite attraction is and why.

When groups are finished, have them read Romans 8:18-25. Have students write on the back of their handouts three ways their knowledge of heaven can affect the way they live their lives now. When the students are ready, have them tell what they wrote. Then say: **Heaven may sound too good to be true, but it's a reality God expects us to take seriously. And just as you've pointed out through your responses, the reality of heaven should affect the way we live today.**

Dream Vacation

Revelation 21:1-7, 15-27

Look at the "attractions" below, and read the verses from Revelation where they're spoken of. Then pick the top three attractions you'd want to visit on a vacation to heaven, and rank them in order of importance to you. Be ready to tell which attraction is your favorite and why you picked it.

Visit the New Jerusalem! Imagine these awesome attractions...

Set Sail on the Sea That Disappeared! (21:1-5)

Walk the Streets of Gold! (21:21)

Drink from the Spring of the Water of Life! (21:6-7)

Touch the Foundation of Precious Stones! (21:15-20)

See the Gates Made From a Single Pearl! (21:21)

Meet God Almighty! (21:22)

Experience the Land of No Night! (21:23-27)

Big Trouble

Purpose:

Teenagers will learn how their faith can help others deal with tragedy.

Supplies:

You'll need Bibles, enough copies of the "Big Trouble" handout (p. 21) so each person can have one of the Mayor's Report boxes cut apart from those handouts, index cards, and pencils.

Experience:

Have students form a circle. Say: **For the next few minutes, each of you will become a mayor of a major city. You'll each receive a description of your city. The description includes whether a disaster has befallen your city and what your reaction to the disaster (or lack of it) will be. Read your description, and then talk with other mayors as you try to meet the goal described on your handout.**

Give each person one of the Mayor's Report boxes cut apart from the "Big Trouble" handout (p. 21). Be sure at least one of each box is distributed. Distribute an equal number of each Mayor's Report box among your group.

On "go," have students each read their Mayor's Report and go around talking with other cities' mayors. Every minute or so, announce that another twenty-five to one hundred people have died or are homeless in the disaster-ridden cities. After five to six minutes, end the simulation. Then ask:

● **What were you thinking as you read your city's situation?** *(I was confident; I felt frustrated; I was disappointed.)*

● **If your city had just experienced a disaster, what went through your mind?** *(It was unfair; I didn't like it; I knew it'd happen to me.)*

● **What did you learn about other mayors as you talked with them?** *(Some mayors didn't want to help; some were more concerned with why the disaster happened than what to do about it.)*

● **How did you feel about the role you played?** *(I'd rather have been able to help; I felt silly; I liked my role.)*

● **Are the mayors' responses to tragedies like the responses you have to tragedies? How?** *(We all have different responses; sometimes I ask "Why?"; disasters don't bother me much.)*

Say: **The tragedies we used for this simulation are the kind we hear about in the news. But smaller tragedies closer to home can actually seem pretty big too.**

Give each student an index card and a pencil. Have each student write one or more tragedies that affect people on a personal level. Kids might list things such as people dying from cancer, victims of gang violence, or traffic accident victims. Collect and read aloud the cards. Ask:

● **Why do these things happen?** *(God lets them happen; people make them happen; I don't know.)*

Say: **We don't always know why things happen, but we can learn how to respond to tragedies such as these. Let's look at the Bible for guidance on how to respond.**

Form two groups, and assign each group a different passage: Ecclesiastes 8:16-17; 9:11-12; or John 9:1-7.

Have groups each read their passage and choose someone to be the "voice" for their group. Say: **I'm going to ask a few questions. After I ask a question, groups each may briefly discuss the question before your voice answers it as if he or she were the author of your Scripture passage.**

Ask groups the following questions:

● **How should we respond to tragedies?** *(We shouldn't just ask why; we should try to help in the healing process; we should trust God to take care of us.)*

● **What role does faith play in dealing with unexpected circumstances?** *(We have to trust that God is in control; our faith helps us overcome difficult times; our faith helps us respond to others in need.)*

● **How would you respond to someone whose close friend or family member dies from cancer?** *(I'd tell him or her we can't understand everything; I'd tell him or her to trust God to help get past the anger and pain.)*

● **How would you respond to a community that's devastated by a hurricane?** *(I'd try to get them to see how faith can help them deal with the situation; I'd help raise money to send to the people in need.)*

Thank the voices for helping with this activity. Then form a circle and ask:

● **Which of the mayors in the simulation we participated in earlier was most like your passage?** *(The questioning role was like Ecclesiastes; the cities that helped were kind of like Jesus helping the blind man.)*

● **Which passage helps us see how we should respond to crises? Explain.** *(The passage in John, because it shows how we can help people who've been affected by tragedy; the passage in Ecclesiastes, because it shows how we can't know why and must rely on faith.)*

Say: **Jesus shows us a faith that heals. Like the disciples and the writer of Ecclesiastes, we can begin to see how our faith can help others deal with tragedy.**

Big Trouble

MAYOR'S REPORT

Event:
Your city has been heavily damaged by a tornado. Many people are homeless and others are dead or injured. Power is out to a large section of town.

Reaction:
Seek a commitment of help from the mayors of cities that haven't experienced a disaster. You'll have to make your plea persuasive in order to count on their assistance. You need the help of at least two other cities.

MAYOR'S REPORT

Event:
Your city has been heavily damaged by a major earthquake. Many people are homeless, and others are dead or injured. Power is out to large sections of town, and fires are raging across the city.

Reaction:
Try to figure out why this earthquake happened and if anyone is at fault for the damage. Approach the other mayors with questions about why such things happen. Question why this had to happen to your city and not someone else's. Don't actively pursue assistance for your city, just ask a lot of "why" questions.

MAYOR'S REPORT

Event:
Your city has enjoyed a wonderful and prosperous year. For years you've worked to save city money for a new multipurpose stadium, and now it looks like you can build it.

Reaction:
Other cities may be experiencing tragedies, but you believe it's best for them to solve their own problems. Besides, none of them wanted to help finance your new stadium! Be tough when others come to you for help.

MAYOR'S REPORT

Event:
Your city has enjoyed a wonderful and prosperous year. For years you've worked to save city money for a badly needed new freeway system. It looks like this may be the year you can build it.

Reaction:
Other cities may be experiencing tragedies, but you believe it's best for them to solve their own problems. Still, you might be convinced to help if the situation is serious. Be aware, though, that you can only help one other city, if you help any at all. The other mayor must have a good case before you help with cleanup (and put off the freeway project).

Build What?

Purpose:

Teenagers will learn to respect the differing views of others.

Supplies:

You'll need Bibles, several sets of dominoes, one photocopy of the "What's My Role?" handout (p. 24) for every three students, one photocopy of the "Spiritual Babies" handout (p. 25) for each person, pencils, tape, newsprint or poster board, and markers.

Experience:

Provide students with several sets of dominoes. Tell students that as a group they are going to construct something out of dominoes.

Photocopy and cut apart enough "What's My Role?" handouts (p. 24) for each person to receive an assignment. Hand them out, and tell students to follow the instructions. Explain that they are not to show their assignments to anyone or share any information from their assignments with anyone.

Allow five to eight minutes for students to work on their constructions. Don't intervene if they begin to disagree and become frustrated with their lack of progress.

When time is up, bring kids together and ask:

● **Did you realize that different members of the group were trying to accomplish different objectives? When?** *(Yes, right after we started; no, I didn't realize that we had different objectives.)*

● **What was it like to try and accomplish the task you were given when others were trying to accomplish something else?** *(It was frustrating; it made me angry.)*

● **How did it feel to play the role you were given?** *(It was hard not to participate; it made me angry, because some people were just doing all the work themselves; it was frustrating to try to lead when no one would follow.)*

● **What made the assignment difficult?** *(We weren't working together; everyone was doing something different.)*

● **How was this activity like problems we experience in the church? at school? at home?** *(Everyone is trying to do something different; people get angry and frustrated with each other.)*

Say: **People in the church, like people everywhere, often come into** the church with their own ideas of how things should be done. Inevitably, personalities will conflict. It was just like that for the people at Corinth. Problems they were having made them feel angry and frustrated. Paul tried to help them find solutions for the things that were dividing them. Let's do the same.

Form three groups. Assign each group one of the following Scripture passages: 1 Corinthians 1:10-13; 1 Corinthians 5:1-8; or 1 Corinthians 6:1-8. Give each group a large sheet of newsprint or poster board and markers. Ask each group to create a poster showing the problem the Corinthian church was dealing with and the solution Paul offered for the problem.

When groups are finished, have them tape their finished posters to the wall. Then have groups each explain their posters to the rest of the class. Ask:

● **What solutions did Paul give for the problems the Corinthian church was experiencing?** *(For everyone to work at agreeing; to have the same mind; to deal with sin in the congregation; to resolve conflict within the church.)*

Give each student a copy of the "Spiritual Babies" handout (p. 25) and a pencil. Ask a volunteer to read aloud 1 Corinthians 3:1-4. Then have students complete the handout.

When everyone is finished, ask volunteers to tell how they responded. Have students discuss any disagreements that arise.

Say: **Sometimes it's hard even for Christians to agree on what a passage like this one is trying to say. But by discussing it openly, we can learn to express our own positions and respect the differing views of others. In this way, we can build unity within diversity.**

What's My Role?

Make enough photocopies of this sheet for each member of your group to have one of the following assignments.

ASSIGNMENT 1

You are a leader in the activity. Lead the group in constructing a tower out of dominoes. You should do your best to involve everyone in the group.

ASSIGNMENT 2

You are a passive observer in the activity. Do not participate in any way.

ASSIGNMENT 3

You are to lead the group in building a house out of dominoes. Allow a few others to help you, but you should do most of the work yourself.

ASSIGNMENT 4

You are to aid others in building the dominoes construction. Try to be as helpful as you can.

Spiritual Babies

"Brothers, I could not address you as spiritual but as worldly—mere infants in Christ. I gave you milk, not solid food, for you were not yet ready for it. Indeed, you are still not ready. You are still worldly. For since there is jealousy and quarreling among you, are you not worldly? Are you not acting like mere men? For when one says, 'I follow Paul,' and another, 'I follow Apollos,' are you not mere men?"
(1 Corinthians 3:1-4).

Circle the response or responses that you think best explains the main ideas of 1 Corinthians 3:1-4.

1 The spiritual milk that Paul spoke of was…

A. food for immature believers to gum.
B. specially blessed goat milk.
C. the Bible.
D. simple truths of the Christian faith.

2 You can tell a believer is immature by…

A. their Christian ID card.
B. how they live their lives.
C. how they get along with other Christians.
D. how much time they spend at church.

3 When believers get into quarrels…

A. it hurts the body of Christ.
B. it shows the immaturity of the believers.
C. it should be resolved by the church.
D. both sides are sinning in some way.

4 Spiritual meat is…

A. the Bible.
B. not for everyone.
C. significant truths of the Christian faith.
D. what you need to keep growing.

5 Acting "worldly"…

A. is what all people really do, isn't it?
B. does not apply to teenagers.
C. means being less than Christ made us.
D. means doing the same things non-Christians do.

6 When Christians argue over which leader to follow…

A. they misunderstand Christ's lordship.
B. they need to all agree on one leader.
C. it is hard to get anything done.
D. they slow down the work of the church.

Calvin Ball

Purpose:

Students will explore the laws the Israelites had to follow and discover how Jesus paid the penalty for all the laws we break.

Supplies:

You'll need Bibles, newsprint, markers, and a ball of any size.

Experience:

Form two teams, and bring out a ball of any size.

Say: **In the classic Calvin and Hobbes comic strip, the two main characters play a game in which they make up all the rules as they go. The object of the game we're about to play is to get the ball across the goal line—as in football—but you'll make up the rules.**

Have the students quickly think up ten creative rules—the crazier the better! (For example, you must have an elbow on the ground to pass or you can run only on your knees.) Write the rules for Calvin Ball on newsprint with a marker. The group must also decide what the penalties will be and who will enforce them. This should be done quickly to allow more time for actual play.

Play Calvin Ball for five minutes.

Gather the group together.

Ask:

● **What was the hardest thing about this game?** *(Following the rules; remembering all the rules.)*

● **How did you feel when you broke a rule?** *(Bad, because I was making us lose; fine, because no one remembered the rules anyway.)*

● **How are the feelings you experienced playing this game like the emotions you feel when you have to "play by the rules" in real life?** *(I'm looking for ways to get around some rules; sometimes it's hard to remember what rules you're supposed to follow.)*

● **Were the rules of this game fair? Why or why not?** *(Yes, no one had an advantage; no, they gave an advantage to tall people.)*

● **How is this game like real life?** *(There are a lot of rules; I can't follow all the rules at the same time; people sometimes get away with breaking the rules.)*

● **How do you feel about people who make or enforce the laws?** *(I feel guilty around them; I don't like them because they always watch to see if I'm doing something wrong.)*

Say: **After the Israelites left Egypt, they had no laws or penalties. God took Moses up on Mount Sinai and told him the laws the Israelites would have to follow. Let's explore some of these laws to see how they apply to us.**

Have a student read aloud Exodus 20:1-17. (If you feel this is too long, briefly summarize the Ten Commandments.) Ask volunteers to reword each commandment into a brief sentence.

Say: **After God gave the Israelites the Ten Commandments, he gave them many more specific laws relating to how people were to treat their servants, what they should do if someone hurt or murdered another person, how thieves should be punished, and other laws governing social and civic situations. These laws were followed by religious laws that the Israelites were supposed to follow.**

Ask students to form teams of two, and have a person read aloud Exodus 23:1-9.

Say: **Some of you may feel as if the laws given in the Bible don't relate to you—as if they were for people who lived thousands of years ago. I'm going to read several different situations, and I want you and your partner to decide what the outcome should be based on the laws we've read today. The first team to answer with the correct outcome based on these laws and can tell where in our Scriptures for today these laws are found, wins that round.**

SITUATION ONE: **There's a girl at school who you know stole your homework and turned it in as her own, but you can't prove it. On the bus after school you find her purse with a bunch of steamy notes from her boyfriend in it. You're tempted to have the notes published in the school newspaper. What should you do, and what law supports your decision?** *(Give them back to her—Exodus 20:15; 23:4.)*

SITUATION TWO: **Your parents want you to go to church on Sunday, but you have a job and have to work. The money you're earning is going toward a paint job and a new stereo for your car. Should you listen to your parents?** *(The car should not come before God—Exodus 20:3; work for six days and keep the other for God and rest—Exodus 20:8-10; obey your parents—Exodus 20:12.)*

SITUATION THREE: **You've wanted a new stereo for months. You've picked out the exact brand and model and tell everyone you want it for your birthday. You don't get the stereo, but your best friend buys it for himself! You're so mad that you stay in your room all day wishing the stereo was yours instead of his. How should you treat your friend?** *(Stop sulking and be glad for him—Exodus 20:17.)*

SITUATION FOUR: **You broke your parents' VCR and didn't tell anyone. Your brother found it broken. It would be easy to tell your parents that he was the one who broke it, since you weren't even home when he tried to use it. What do you do?** *(Be truthful—Exodus 20:16; 23:1.)*

SITUATION FIVE: **You don't use dirty or obscene language, but most of your friends say "God!" to express frustration or anger. Is this wrong?** *(Don't misuse the name of the Lord—Exodus 20:7.)*

Total up each team's points, and declare a winner.

Say: **A lot of the situations we get into relate to the laws God gave so long ago. But who can remember all these rules and regulations? Religious leaders always tried to trick Jesus into making a mistake. Once they asked him what the most important commandment was. Let's hear how he answered.**

Have a volunteer read aloud Mark 12:28-31.

Ask:

● **Is this a good summary of all the commandments?** *(Yes, if you follow these laws you won't break any others; not really—sometimes you love people so much you do something wrong, such as lie to protect them.)*

● **Is it possible for most people to follow these laws?** *(No, that's why we need God's forgiveness; yes, these are simple laws.)*

Say: **Jesus made the laws easier for us to remember and, even better, he paid the penalty for all the laws we break. We don't have to murder someone to be lawbreakers. Just thinking a mean thought makes us a lawbreaker! And that means a penalty. But Christ's death and resurrection paid that penalty for us. We just have to acknowledge our lawbreaking habits and ask for his forgiveness.**

Cereal Swallowers

Purpose:

Teenagers will learn how to trust God.

Supplies:

You'll need Bibles, chairs, blindfolds, spoons, bowls of cold cereal, one photocopy of the "Map It Out" handout (p. 31) for each person, and pencils.

Experience:

Have teenagers each choose a partner. Have one partner sit on a chair and the other stand behind the chair. Have each person who's standing put on a blindfold and hold a spoon.

Give each person sitting down a bowl of cold cereal. Be sure they hold the bowls in front of them.

Say: **This is a race to see which person can eat all of his or her cereal first. The person who's standing must feed the person who's sitting. You cannot touch each other—no holding the hand of the person feeding you—and you cannot spill cereal onto the floor. Begin!**

Watch to be sure no team breaks the rules. When a team wins, congratulate the winners.

Ask:

● **How did you who were sitting react during this activity?** *(I didn't trust my partner; after awhile, I trusted my partner to feed me correctly.)*

● **What did you who were standing think about during this activity?** *(My partner complained too much; frustrated that I couldn't do a better job.)*

● **What made it hard to trust your partner?** *(He kept dropping cereal on me; I knew she couldn't see.)*

● **How is trying to trust your partner like trusting God?** *(I trusted my partner to tell me where his mouth was, and I trust God to lead me; I didn't think my partner was giving me very much help, and I don't think God helps me very much.)*

Say: **Trusting God is difficult because we can't always see where he's leading us. We often feel as if we're just supposed to blindly trust God. "If only God would clearly show me the way," we complain. The Israelites in Exodus struggled with the same problem.**

Give each student a copy of the "Map It Out" handout and a pencil. Have students form groups of three, and give each group a Bible. Ask the groups each to complete the first section of the handout together. Tell students they should each work on the second section alone.

After they've completed the handouts, ask volunteers to tell about their own "personal future" map. Then say: **Sometimes we think we can plan out our lives pretty easily. Yet we often encounter more mountains and valleys than we plan for.**

Ask:

● **Why does God allow us to go through hard times?** *(Sometimes trials help us see how powerful God is; I see how trials can help make me stronger.)*

● **Do hard times make it harder to trust God? Why or why not?** *(Yes, because I'm not sure he's really looking out for me; no, I think my faith grows stronger during hard times.)*

Say: **Sometimes we think it was easy for people in the Bible to trust in God, but they were people just like you and me. As you look at the map you drew, you know there will be changes. One way to build our trust in God is to follow what's written in the Bible. Another way is to remember how God has helped us in the past—which gives us strength to trust him in the present.**

Map It Out

Section 1:

(Do this in your group.) Below is a map of the area written about in Exodus. The Israelites were captives in Egypt, and God had promised to give them the land of Canaan. If you were Moses, how would you plan the journey from Egypt to Canaan? Chart your course on the map.

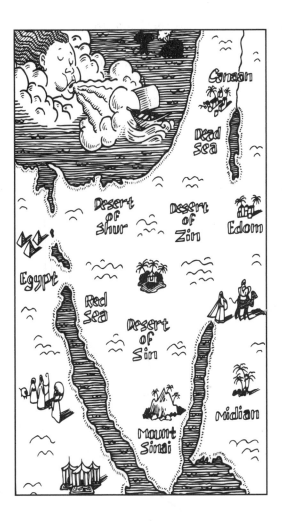

Now read the following verses, and chart the actual course the Israelites took: Exodus 13:17-18, 20-22; 14:1-4, 21-22. Then discuss the following questions.

● Why did God lead the Israelites by a longer route?

● Why did God lead the Israelites to the Red Sea when he knew the Egyptians were right behind them?

● How would you have felt if you were wandering around with Moses?

● How do you think the Israelites felt? (Exodus 14:10-14 gives you a clue!)

Section 2:

(Do this on your own.) Now make a map of your future as *you* think it should happen. Add more landmarks to reflect how you see your future today.

Choice Chairs

Purpose:
Teenagers will learn that God has shown us all we need to know to get to heaven.

Supplies:
You'll need Bibles, masking tape, paper, pencils, chairs, snacks, and a copy of the "Wheat or Weed?" handout (p. 34) for each group of four or five.

Experience:
Before class, put a small piece of masking tape out of sight on the bottom of about one-third of the chairs. Write "heaven" on one sheet of paper and "hell" on another. Tape these signs on opposite ends of the room.

When it's time for this activity, have students form a circle with their chairs. Place snacks under the "heaven" sign.

Have students each look under their chair and remove the tape if it's there.

Say: **Those of you who have a piece of tape get to go to heaven. Please take your chair, and move over next to the sign marked "heaven." Enjoy the snacks. Those of you who have no tape must go to hell. Please stand next to the sign marked "hell."**

When students are in place, ask:

● **What's it like standing or sitting where you are?** *(It's boring over here in hell; I'm glad I found the tape so I could have the food.)*

● **How is this activity similar to the way we end up in either heaven or hell?** *(It isn't, because it was just a random choice; we don't actually decide where we go.)*

● **How is this activity different?** *(We had no choice in this activity; whether we go to heaven is based on our faith, not on a random choice.)*

● **If the pieces of tape represented making a faith commitment to Jesus, how would that change your view of this activity?** *(Then it makes sense, since those who have faith in Jesus go to heaven; it still isn't right, since those with the tape were just lucky.)*

Say: **God does ultimately decide who will enter his heaven, but he has provided all the information we need to get there.**

Have the students in "heaven" share the snacks with the rest of the class.

Form four groups, and give each group the "Wheat or Weed?" handout (p. 34), a pencil, and a Bible. Assign each group one section of the handout.

Have groups each read Matthew 13:24-30, 36-43 and John 3:14-18, and then complete their section of the handout based on the information in the passages.

When groups are finished, have them explain their answers and ask other students whether or not they agree. Allow several minutes for open discussion. Then ask:

● **Does the Bible give easy answers about who will go to heaven? Why or why not?** *(No, it doesn't talk about other religions much; yes, it's clear only people who believe in Jesus will get to heaven.)*

● **Why do you think we don't have easy answers to these situations?** *(God is in control, and he just lets us know what we need to know; we don't know the whole situation.)*

● **How does the "gray area" concerning who will go to heaven affect the way you live your life?** *(I want to be sure I'm going, so I'll stay away from things I'm not sure about; I want to help people who are living in the gray areas.)*

● **Based on what we've read so far in the Bible, who will go to heaven?** *(Those who believe in Jesus and follow him; those who turn away from doing bad things and live for God.)*

Say: **Rather than worrying about what we don't know, we need to make sure we aren't ignoring what we do know about going to heaven. Through Jesus and the Word, God has shown us all we need to know to get to heaven. But we must decide to listen and live by what he has said.**

Wheat or Weed?

In your group, read Matthew 13:24-30, 36-43, and John 3:14-18. Then read your assigned situation below and decide, based on the passages, if it would be easy, difficult, or impossible for you to determine whether that person will go to heaven. Then talk about why you chose what you did for each situation.

Lakshmi is a Hindu teenager living in India. She worships three gods: Brahma, Siva, and Vishnu. She has been taught that her gods are manifestations of the one "all-pervading substance" of the universe (Brahman), which is like a god but is impersonal. She believes she is destined to live life on earth many times before she becomes pure enough to be reunited with Brahman. Will Lakshmi go to heaven?

EASY   **DIFFICULT**   **IMPOSSIBLE**

Bill wandered into a revival meeting held in his hometown one night. At the end of the meeting, he prayed a prayer something like this: "I believe in Jesus as my personal Savior." As he looks back on the experience with a grin, he wonders what ever got him to pray something like that. All that wimpy stuff is behind him now. Will Bill go to heaven?

EASY   **DIFFICULT**   **IMPOSSIBLE**

Jill is always in church! She is president of her youth group and serves on five different committees. Jill takes pride in being thought of as someone who walks close to God. In fact, she once confided in a friend that she thought God was pretty lucky to have her. Will Jill go to heaven?

EASY   **DIFFICULT**   **IMPOSSIBLE**

Professor Bultwynn teaches classes in theology at the big seminary downtown. He knows just about everything that could be known about Christianity and deep theological issues. That's why it surprises some of his students when they see the big mural on his office wall that says, "The most profound truth ever spoken is 'Jesus loves me, this I know; for the Bible tells me so.' " Will Professor Bultwynn go to heaven?

EASY   **DIFFICULT**   **IMPOSSIBLE**

Choose Your Punishment

Purpose:

Students will explore what the Bible says about hell.

Supplies:

You'll need Bibles, a copy of the "Punishments" handout (p. 37), tape, pencils, and one copy of the "Three Who Don't Make It" handout (p. 38) for each person.

Experience:

Say: **Hell isn't a subject to be taken lightly. But to help us understand the implications of hell, we're going to look at a fictional situation.**

Photocopy and cut apart the punishments listed in the "Punishments" handout (p. 37). Or write each punishment on a separate index card.

Have students form a circle, and then read aloud this scenario: **You were warned repeatedly that you could *not* have another cookie. But in a moment of extreme temptation, you slipped into the kitchen, reached into the cookie jar, and pulled out two chocolate chip cookies.**

You thought about putting them back, but then you heard someone coming, so you stuffed the cookies into your mouth and headed for the back door. Suddenly a booming voice said: "I saw that! I am the Cookie King. Choose your punishment!" After the Cookie King gives you your choices, you must choose which punishment the person to your right must suffer.

Pick six people to hold the slips of paper listing the punishments. Challenge your class to rank the punishments from "worst" to "least bad."

Allow students several minutes to discuss how the punishments should be ranked. Once the order is decided, tape the slips to the wall from worst (on the left) to least bad (on the right). Then have students each choose the punishment for the person on their right by moving that person to stand in front of the appropriate punishment. Once everyone has been assigned a punishment, ask:

● **How do you feel about your punishment? Explain.** *(Awful, it seems too severe; OK, it's not one of the worst punishments.)*

● **How did you feel about assigning a punishment? Explain.** *(OK, until I saw that other people got easier punishments; bad, I didn't want to make the person mad at me.)*

● **Is this the way hell is? Why or why not?** *(No, because the punishment is the same for everyone; yes, because we all get punished for what we do.)*

● **Do you think it's fair for some people to go to hell and others to go to heaven? Why or why not?** *(Yes, because they made the choices that led them there; no, everyone should be treated the same.)*

● **Does God arbitrarily assign a punishment for each person on earth, just as we did in this activity? Why or why not?** *(No, God treats each person according to what he or she deserves; no, people condemn themselves by their actions; yes, it's all a matter of luck who gets into heaven.)*

Say: **"No-cookie hell" may not be much like the real hell, but it gives us a chance to feel what it might be like to be condemned because of our actions—even actions we may think are OK. Now let's take a look at what the Bible says about the real hell and who goes there.**

Give each student the "Three Who Don't Make It" handout (p. 38) and a pencil. Form three groups, assign each group one section of the handout, and give each group a Bible. Have groups read through the passages and work together to complete their sections of the handout.

When groups are finished, have them tell what they wrote. After all the groups have shared, ask:

● **What do these three situations tell you about hell?** *(It's hot; it's a place of condemnation.)*

● **What do these three situations tell you about who goes to hell?** *(Selfish people; Satan; those who don't believe in Jesus.)*

● **Based on these passages, do you think God *sends* people to hell? Why or why not?** *(Yes, if they deserve it; no, people condemn themselves by their own choices.)*

Say: **It's not clear exactly what hell is like. But it's certainly not a place we want to live. People in heaven will spend eternity with God, which will never be boring. But "eternity" is also the word the Bible sometimes uses to describe the fate of those destined for hell. By knowing Christ, we're sure to avoid that terrible fate.**

The Punishments

- Go to no-cookie hell: Be separated from cookies forever.

- Have your taste buds surgically removed.

- Eat six cookies—and drink a quart of milk that has been sitting in the sun for two weeks.

- Bake in the cookie oven until you're light and crispy.

- Have flour sprinkled on your eyeballs.

- Go to school with a stick of butter in each shoe.

Three Who Don't Make It

Have someone in your group read aloud the passage assigned to your group. Then answer the questions in the appropriate section of the handout.

The Selfish Rich Man (Luke 16:19-31)

- Why is this man in hell?
- What might have kept this person out of hell?
- How does this example apply to your life?

The Lover of Darkness (John 3:16-21)

- Why are some people judged guilty?
- What does it mean to love darkness rather than light?
- Are people punished with hell, or do they choose it for themselves?

The Devil (Revelation 20:1-3, 7-10)

- What is the "lake of burning sulfur" used for?
- Does Satan's punishment seem fair to you? Why or why not?
- Why do you think God created hell, based on this passage?

The Cost of Giving

Purpose:

Students will explore how important a right attitude is when giving gifts to others.

Supplies:

You'll need Bibles and five pennies for each group member. Also, prepare a "gift" bag of common household or office items such as pencils, tape dispensers, books, and silverware.

Experience:

Make sure you have enough items in the gift bags for each of your students. Don't include anything breakable or valuable.

Give each person five pennies. Tell students they're going to play a game and the game will have two rounds.

For round one, instruct group members they'll have two minutes to get as many pennies as they can. They can use any method except stealing, but they should try to end up with more pennies than they started with. Students can offer to do favors for others in exchange for pennies or even sell their shoes.

This activity can get wild, so remind students to be careful not to hurt each other.

Give the signal to start, and after two minutes call time. Find out how many kids ended up with more pennies than they started with.

Ask:

● **What emotions did you experience as you were trying to get as many pennies as you could from everyone else?** *(I felt powerful; I felt like I wanted to win at any cost; I felt embarrassed.)*

● **How is that like the way people feel about receiving gifts at Christmas?** *(They feel selfish about getting things; they feel embarrassed about getting gifts.)*

● **How did you feel about the people around you who were trying to get as many pennies as they could from you?** *(It was part of the game; I was upset they were so greedy.)*

For round two, have students divide up the pennies so each person has five again. Tell kids this time the object is to give away all of their pennies. Tell students they can only give away one penny at a time, and no one may refuse to receive a penny when it is offered to him or her. Give students two minutes to get rid of their pennies. When two minutes are up, call time and find out how many got rid of all their pennies. Also find out how many ended up with more pennies than they started with.

Ask:

● **How did the feeling in the room change for you during this part of the activity?** *(It seemed to be more relaxed; it was more fun.)*

● **What was it like trying to give pennies away?** *(I felt generous; it was better than when I was trying to get them from others.)*

● **How is this like the way you feel when you give gifts to others at Christmas?** *(I feel good when I give others presents; I feel worthwhile when I do something nice for someone.)*

● **What did you think about the others while they were trying to give you pennies?** *(I thought they might win the game; they were pretty nice.)*

● **What does this game tell you about people's attitudes at Christmastime?** *(Lots of people are trying to get rather than give; Christmas must be really stressful for greedy people.)*

Say: **When our attitude is right, giving gifts at Christmas can be fun and rewarding.**

Have each student pull a "gift" out of the gift bag you prepared earlier. After each person pulls out an item, have him or her give the item to someone else in the class and tell why he or she chose that person. For example, someone might say, "I give you this gift because I value your friendship" or "I give you this gift because you're kind to others." Tell students no person may receive more than one gift.

After all the students have received their gifts, tell them to work together to create a nativity scene using only the items they've been given. Allow five minutes for students to complete the project. Encourage them to include a stable, a manger, animals, Mary and Joseph, angels, and wise men. If your group is larger than twelve, form smaller groups of no more than ten to independently complete this activity.

When students are finished, examine their work, praising students for the parts of the nativity you understand and asking students to explain the parts you don't. Then ask:

● **What went through your mind when I asked you to make a nativity out of your gifts?** *(I felt stupid; I didn't think it could be done.)*

● **What do you think of your nativity now that it's finished?** *(It doesn't look much like a nativity to me; it turned out better than I expected.)*

● **Why was it hard to make a nativity out of the gifts you were**

given? *(They weren't the right size or shape; they had nothing to do with Jesus' birth.)*

● **How is this nativity like what happens when people focus on gifts rather than on Jesus' birth?** *(The real meaning of Christmas gets obscured by all the products; it makes the Christmas story look cheap.)*

Say: **Gifts are fun and giving gifts can be fun. But often what makes a gift valuable is the attitudes of the people involved. Are they giving to celebrate Christ's birth? Or are they giving just because everyone else is? Let's take a look at our attitudes and the attitudes of some characters involved in the first Christmas.**

Ask for volunteers to read aloud the following Scripture passages: Matthew 2:1-12; Luke 2:8-20; and 2 Corinthians 9:7.

● **In each passage, what were the gifts given?** *(In Matthew 2:1-12, the wise men gave gifts of gold, incense, and myrrh to Jesus; in Luke 2:8-20, the angels gave the shepherds the gift of God's message; the shepherds gave the gift of their worship to Jesus; the Luke passage talks about God giving the gift of Jesus to the world; in 2 Corinthians 9:7, Paul talked about giving gifts cheerfully to others.)*

● **From what we just read, what was the motive of the "givers"?** *(They wanted to honor God; they wanted to show love to others.)*

● **How would you apply 2 Corinthians 9:7 to Christmas?** *(Maybe it's not worth giving a gift if you feel pressured into it; you should enjoy giving gifts.)*

Say: **It's easy for us to focus on the "getting" angle of Christmas. But everybody at the first Christmas—God, the angels, the shepherds, the wise men—seemed to be working harder at giving to others. Not all of them gave the kind of gifts you can go to a store to buy. They were gifts of the heart—the kind of gifts any of us can give.**

Daring Decisions

Purpose:

Students will learn that God doesn't ask us to do things that we aren't capable of doing.

Supplies:

You'll need Bibles; index cards; a pen; and a bag of goodies, such as healthy cookies.

Experience:

Before the meeting, write the words "Risk Card" on each card in a stack of index cards (you'll need three cards for every participant).

Give each person three Risk Cards. Explain that you'll read a risky situation, and those who are willing to take the risk must stand up and give you one Risk Card (more than one person may turn in a Risk Card at a time). You'll then read the outcome, and each student who has taken a risk will receive either a reward (a cookie) or a penalty. Students must each use all of their Risk Cards or they'll receive a penalty at the end of the game. (Don't tell your students how many situations you'll be reading.)

SITUATION ONE: **You want to ask the best-looking girl or guy in your school to go out. If you're willing to risk being turned down, stand up and turn in a Risk Card.**

OUTCOME: **You get turned down! Everyone who took the risk must do ten jumping jacks.**

SITUATION TWO: **Your science teacher is lecturing on evolution. He says he can't believe anyone would be stupid enough to believe in the creation account in the Bible. You want to tell him you think he's wrong, but you're afraid everyone will laugh at you. If you're willing to disagree publicly with the teacher, stand and turn in a Risk Card.**

OUTCOME: **The teacher thinks you're wrong, and the class seems to agree. Later the guy who sits behind you asks you a question about God. He agrees to come to church with you. You have to do three push-ups, but you also get two rewards because the embarrassment was worth it.**

SITUATION THREE: You want to try out for a sports team but are afraid you won't make the team. If you want to go for it, stand and turn in a Risk Card.

OUTCOME: You don't make the team! Everyone who took the risk must sing "Mary Had a Little Lamb."

SITUATION FOUR: Your best friend ditched school yesterday and wants you to write an absence excuse. If you're caught, you'll get suspended. But you're afraid to turn down your friend. Stand up and turn in a Risk Card if you're willing to write the note.

OUTCOME: Your friend gets caught when the school calls his mother. He doesn't tell on you, but you feel so guilty you confess. You get detention. In this situation, there is no punishment or reward.

SITUATION FIVE: Your boyfriend or girlfriend is pressuring you to have sex. You're afraid of a break-up if you don't give in. If you're willing to say no, stand and turn in a Risk Card.

OUTCOME: Your boyfriend or girlfriend breaks up with you. However, you know you did the best thing. You get a reward.

SITUATION SIX: A popular girl wants to copy your homework. You feel as if she's just using you, but you're afraid she'll spread rumors about you if you don't agree. If you'd turn her down, stand and turn in a Risk Card.

OUTCOME: She's mad. But after school she apologizes and asks if you'll help her study. You say yes, and get a reward.

At this point, anyone who still has one or more Risk Cards must stand and pay the penalty for not taking any risks. They must sing "Row, Row, Row Your Boat" complete with rowing motions.

Ask:

● **What went through your mind when you knew you had to take a risk?** (I didn't know if I should do it; I was afraid of the penalty.)

● **How were the situations and results like real life? How were they different?** (I usually feel rewarded when I do the right thing; it's not always true that people who do the wrong thing get punished and those who do the right thing get a reward.)

● **How do you decide whether a risk is worth taking?** (I think about whether it's the right thing to do or not; I go on a gut feeling.)

● **What are some situations you'd feel afraid to take a risk in?** (Asking someone out who's going out with someone else; confronting a friend who's done something wrong.)

● **What's one situation where the risk might be worth taking, but could have a bad outcome?** *(Learning to drive; telling others about your faith in Christ.)*

Say: **God once chose a man named Moses to take some life-and-death risks on behalf of his people. And Moses wasn't all that thrilled about doing what God asked him to. Let's learn how he overcame his fears.**

Ask volunteers to read aloud Exodus 3:7-14; 4:1; and 6:30.

Say: **The Israelites were slaves to the Egyptians. God asked Moses to approach Pharaoh (who was like a king) and tell him to let all these people go free.**

Ask:

● **How would you have responded to God?** *(Just like Moses did—with fear; I would have obeyed, knowing that God would protect me.)*

Say: **Regardless of what you would've done, Moses had a real decision to make. Would he risk his life to obey God? Maybe we can understand some of Moses' emotions by imagining this classroom is "Egypt" and I'm now your "Pharaoh."**

Form groups of three or more. Assign each group a different work task. These tasks should be useful but somewhat unpleasant, such as dusting pews or chairs in your sanctuary, picking up litter around the church, or straightening the nursery.

Say: **Each group has an important task to do, but I'll allow one group freedom from their task. Choose one person from your group to come before me, your Pharaoh. That person must explain why your group chose him or her to come before me, why your group deserves freedom, and why I should listen to him or her.**

Give the groups two minutes to prepare their case.

Have each group send a representative to you. Question each one briefly. Select one group to be set free.

As the other groups moan and complain, ask:

● **What are your reactions to my choice?** *(I'm disappointed, it doesn't seem fair; I'm angry at our representative.)*

● **How are your feelings like the feelings the Israelites had under Pharaoh's rule? How are they different?** *(I bet they were as frustrated as we are; our task isn't like the slavery they experienced.)*

● **How did the group representatives feel as you presented your case?** *(Nervous, I was afraid of letting my group down; confident, I thought you'd choose us.)*

● **How do you think Moses must have felt asking for freedom for hundreds of thousands of people who were doing hard physical labor?** *(Afraid; intimidated.)*

Send off all the groups (except the one you set free) to do their tasks for four minutes. When they return, say: **Pharaoh turned Moses down ten times! Each time Moses told Pharaoh if he didn't let the people of Israel go, God would punish him. And God did. He sent ten different plagues to punish Pharaoh's people. But God shielded the Israelites from the plagues because Moses risked obeying him. And each time Pharaoh turned down Moses, Moses was taking the risk that more of his people were going to suffer and die. Finally Pharaoh let the Israelites go.**

Ask:

● **Do you think God would ask you to do something you couldn't do?** *(Yes, sometimes God seems to ask the impossible; no, I think God helps us do what he asks us to.)*

Say: **When God asks us to do something, we may not feel capable to do it, but God believes that each of us is able to do his will.**

Deduction Junction

Purpose:

Teenagers will learn how to have confidence in the evidence and facts that support Jesus' resurrection.

Supplies:

You'll need Bibles, index cards, a photocopy of the "Body Search" handout (p. 49), and pencils.

Experience:

Before the meeting, photocopy and cut apart the "Body Search" handout (p. 49) as directed.

For this activity, you'll need ten index cards for each team. Number each set of cards one through ten on one side only. Shuffle each card set.

Form teams of no more than six. Have students number themselves one to six. (If a team has less than six members, some students will need to take two numbers.) Across from each team place a set of cards face down on the floor in a pile.

Say: **The object of this game is for each team member to find the card with his or her number on it. When it's your turn, run to the set of cards and turn over a card. If it's the correct number, take the card, and then quickly mix the cards and again lay them face down before returning to your team. If it's not correct, do ten jumping jacks then turn another card over. Continue until you find the right card. Then mix the cards, and turn them face down for the next person. The first team to have all members find their correct cards wins.**

Begin the activity. Monitor students as they turn over cards to be sure no one cheats. Also be sure the person mixing the cards doesn't try to place them in a specific order for the next team member.

Congratulate the team that finishes first, and have all students sit down. Ask:

● **What was it like trying to pick the right card on the first try?** *(I felt hopeless because there was no way to know which one it was; I felt lucky because I guessed right.)*

● **What were you thinking as more cards in your set were eliminated?** *(I was still frustrated; I was more confident because my odds of finding the right card were increasing.)*

● **Why were you more likely to find the right card after several tries?** *(The odds were more in my favor; even if I didn't know which card to pick, I at least knew which cards not to pick.)*

● **How was this game like the way we determine our beliefs concerning Jesus' resurrection? How was it different?** *(The more we know, the more wrong answers we can eliminate; the more we know about what not to believe, the more confident we can be that our faith's correct.)*

Say: **Just as there were many different cards for you to choose from, there are many different theories about what actually happened after Jesus died. Let's look at them and, as in this game, find the right answer by getting rid of the wrong answers.**

Form four groups. Give each group one section of the handout and a pencil.

Have each group determine which member will be the informant (reading to the group), the pen pusher (taking notes on the discussion), and the agent (speaking for the group during questioning). All other members will be promoters (making sure each person participates).

(If groups have less than four members, have students take more than one role.)

Say: **I've given you some of the most common theories about what happened after Jesus died. Together read the theory, and list reasons why this theory could be true or why it could be false.**

Leader Tip

If groups have more than six members, form eight or more groups. Photocopy the handout as needed, ensuring each theory is represented at least once.

After a couple minutes have groups read Matthew 28:1-15 together.

Say: **Continue your discussion, taking into account this new information.**

Allow several minutes for discussion, then have the agent for the swoon theory share the group's theory and conclusions. Ask:

● **What happened to Jesus before he was hung on the cross?** *(He was beaten; he was whipped.)*

● **If Jesus hadn't died, what might his condition have been like after this treatment?** *(He'd be half-dead; he'd be weak; he'd be helpless.)*

● **Could a person in this condition roll a huge and heavy stone away from the tomb's opening?** *(No, it wouldn't be possible; he'd be too weak.)*

Say: **Another problem with this theory is that John 19:34 says a soldier thrust a spear into Jesus' side to be sure he was dead. Blood and water came out of this wound, showing Jesus had been dead long enough for his bodily fluids to separate from his blood.**

Ask:

● **Is there enough evidence for you to believe this theory? If so, explain.** *(Yes, because he's the Son of God; no, because no one could survive that treatment.)*

Have the agent for the vision theory share the group's theory and conclusions. Ask:

● **If it was just a hallucination, why don't those who support this theory show us Jesus' body?** *(They can't find it; it's long gone; because Jesus came back to life.)*

● **Most of Jesus' followers who claimed to have seen Jesus alive were later tortured and killed. If they made up this story, why were so many willing to die for what they had said?** *(They were crazy; they were telling the truth; they had told the story so long they all believed it.)*

● **Is there enough evidence for you to believe this theory? If so, explain.** *(Yes, because lots of people hallucinate when they're grieving; no, because Jesus said it would happen.)*

Have the agent for the deceptive disciples theory share. Ask:

● **How did these disciples, who hid during the Crucifixion, suddenly have the courage to sneak past the Roman guards?** *(They gathered together for a pep talk; they were still afraid and in hiding.)*

● **How could the guards fall so soundly asleep that they couldn't hear the stone being rolled away?** *(It had been a long day; they were on drugs.)*

● **Why would the guards be so careless when they knew they could be executed if the body was stolen?** *(They weren't paying attention; there really was an angel, and they passed out from fear.)*

Say: **Again, there's the question of why the disciples would all stick to their story even though they were tortured and put to death. You'd think at least *one* of them would've changed his story if it were all a lie!**

Ask:

● **Is there enough evidence for you to believe this theory? If so, explain.** *(Yes, because the disciples had been deceptive before; no, because they wouldn't risk their lives.)*

Have the agent for the risen Savior theory share. Ask:

● **What problems do you have believing this theory?** *(A person simply can't come back to life; I don't have a problem with it.)*

● **What are reasons for believing this theory?** *(God is powerful enough to do anything; it follows the prophecies about Jesus' death; it follows what Jesus said would happen.)*

● **After considering the evidence for these various theories, what do you think about the claim that Jesus rose from the dead?** *(I'm more confident in my belief; I feel stronger in my faith; I'm relieved.)*

Say: **We can have intelligent and confident faith in the Resurrection because the facts support it. And with the guidance of the Holy Spirit, we can learn to trust and accept Jesus' sacrifice for our sins.**

Body Search

Photocopy this handout, and cut it into four sections. (For larger groups photocopy as needed.)

One way to prove Jesus is not God is to explain why his tomb was empty. If Christ is not risen, then where was his body?

The Swoon Theory

This theory suggests that Christ did not actually die on the cross, but only "swooned" or fainted. Thinking he was dead, the soldiers placed Jesus in the tomb. When he revived, he left the tomb and appeared to his followers.

One way to prove Jesus is not God is to explain why his tomb was empty. If Christ is not risen, then where was his body?

The Vision Theory

This theory suggests that Jesus' followers believed he had come back to life because they were hallucinating. The disciples so badly wanted Jesus to be alive that they lost touch with reality and were actually seeing things that weren't there.

One way to prove Jesus is not God is to explain why his tomb was empty. If Christ is not risen, then where was his body?

The Deceptive Disciples Theory

This theory claims the disciples stole Jesus' body and lied when they said he had risen.

One way to prove Jesus is not God is to explain why his tomb was empty. If Christ is not risen, then where was his body?

The Risen Savior Theory

This theory claims Jesus did indeed die and come to life again three days later just as he'd promised. Jesus had the power to do this because he is the Son of God.

Do-It-Yourself Religion

Purpose:

Students will explore why New Age philosophies go against Christianity.

Supplies:

You'll need Bibles, paper, pencils, and photocopies of the "Do It Yourself" handout (p. 53) and the "New Age Beliefs" box (p. 52). Make enough copies so each group of four can have three different cards from the handout.

Experience:

Form groups of no more than four. Give each group paper, pencils, and three different cards from the "Do It Yourself" handout (p. 53). Mix up the cards so groups don't have matching sets of cards. Tell groups they'll each have seven minutes to design a religion based on the information from one or more of their cards. Encourage students to be creative and come up with unusual religions. Let kids use the Bible to find additional verses to support their religions.

As they design their religion, have students keep the following four things in mind:

● The religion must somehow be based on the information from at least one of the cards.

● The religion must help people know the difference between right and wrong.

● The religion must describe who or what its god is and what role that god plays.

● Someone in each group must be able to describe the basic beliefs of the religion in three sentences or less.

After seven minutes, call time. Have representatives from the groups each describe the basic beliefs of their religion in three sentences or less. Allow a couple of minutes for class members to ask questions about any other group's religion.

Then ask:

● **What was it like to design a religion?** *(I felt silly; it was insightful; I didn't like it; it felt wrong.)*

● **What's the attraction of forming your own religion?** *(You set up the rules you like; you can do what you want.)*

● **Who is the god in each of these religions?** *(We are; nobody; everything.)*

● **How do people know the difference between right and wrong in each religion?** *(There are rules to define right and wrong; they don't.)*

● **How are the religions you created like or unlike Christianity?** *(They have some similar beliefs; they don't rely on God.)*

● **How is this exercise like "playing God"?** *(Only God can create religion; when we set our own rules, we're being like God.)*

Say: **When people pick and choose parts of many religions to create their own, they end up playing God. People who believe in New Age ideas like to say that Christianity is important to their beliefs, but they only like parts of Christianity. They may think Jesus was a wonderful teacher, but disbelieve that he was the only Son of God. They might like the principles of Jesus' teaching, but they don't agree with Jesus when he says, "I am the way and the truth and the life. No one comes to the Father except through me."**

Ask:

● **What's so bad about including beliefs besides Christianity in what we believe?** *(It waters down our faith; our faith loses purpose.)*

Say: **When you incorporate ideas from many different religions to create a religion you can feel comfortable with, the end result is separating yourself from God. New Age beliefs state, "I can do all things through me who strengthens me." Christians believe, "I can do all things through Christ who strengthens me." It's a subtle difference in wording—but a major difference in meaning.**

Form groups of no more than four, and assign them either Genesis 3:1-7 or Romans 1:18-25. Give pencils and a copy of the "New Age Beliefs" box (p. 52) to each group.

Say: **The basic New Age beliefs are so "un-new" that they're mentioned in the Bible. In your groups, read your Scripture, and identify the New Age belief or beliefs the verses describe. Then list the verse next to each belief it represents or contradicts on your copy of the "New Age Beliefs" box.**

Allow students five minutes to read and discuss their verses. Here are some matches students might make: Genesis 3:5 with 2, 3, or 4; Genesis 3:6 with 3 or 4; Romans 1:20 with 1; Romans 1:23 with 1 or 2; and Romans 1:25 with 1 or 2.

Have groups each share their findings with the whole group.
Then ask:

● **Why do you think New Age beliefs are so similar to the beliefs described in the Bible?** *(They're not new ideas at all; these beliefs have been a problem for years.)*

● **How do Christians become transformed?** *(By allowing God to act in our lives; by responding to God's desire for us to be changed.)*

● **How is a Christian's transformation different from the transformation described in New Age beliefs?** *(Jesus' return will change the world; Jesus transforms us, we don't do it ourselves.)*

● **Why is it important to know that New Age philosophies are not compatible with Christian faith?** *(Because our faith is weakened if we believe they're OK; it helps us know how to communicate with people who believe New Age teachings.)*

Say: **New Age thinkers have admirable goals—they want to change the world and make it a better place to live. But they try to accomplish those goals without God. As the Scriptures clearly indicate, we can't do anything without God.**

New Age Beliefs

1. God is neither separate nor distinct from creation.

2. People are part of God and thus are divine (like God).

3. Our problem is we don't know we're divine.

4. The solution is personal transformation.

5. Transformation happens through changing how we think.

6. Through reincarnation, we have more than one chance at transformation.

7. When enough people are transformed, the world will change.

Do It Yourself

Copy these cards, and cut them apart. Give three different cards to each group.

"The Lord is my shepherd, I shall not be in want."
—Psalm 23:1

" 'Everything is permissible'—but not everything is beneficial. 'Everything is permissible'—but not everything is constructive."
—1 Corinthians 10:23

"Whoever loves discipline loves knowledge, but he who hates correction is stupid."
—Proverbs 12:1

"You are God in your universe."
—Werner Erhard

" 'Meaningless! Meaningless!' says the Teacher. 'Utterly meaningless! Everything is meaningless.' "
—Ecclesiastes 1:2

"All disease is a question of human consciousness."
—Shirley McLaine

"Jesus turned and saw her. 'Take heart, daughter,' he said, 'your faith has healed you.' And the woman was healed from that moment."
—Matthew 9:22

"There is no need to have rules, regulations, or commandments."
—Shinto belief

"Then Jesus said to his disciples: 'Therefore I tell you, do not worry about your life, what you will eat; or about your body, what you will wear. Life is more than food, and the body more than clothes.' "
—Luke 12:22-23

"God is one with each person."
—Hindu belief

Electric Fence

Purpose:

Students will examine how Joseph's faith in God kept him strong through difficult or seemingly impossible circumstances.

Supplies:

You'll need Bibles, two ladders, heavy rope or twine, index cards, and pencils.

Experience:

Prior to this session, find an open area inside or outside to set up two stand-alone, ten-foot ladders and tie a twenty-foot rope or heavy twine between them at the tops of both ladders. Make sure the ladders don't fall on students. (If you prefer, anchor the rope to opposite walls in your room, at least eight feet up.)

Explain to your class members that they have seven minutes to get every person in class over the rope. Girls in dresses could act as spotters. They must all start on one side and can't go around or under, only over. It's wise to have a couple strong adult helpers on hand (especially to catch the first few students over the rope).

Watch this exercise closely. Take note of which students lead (often it's the athletic ones) and which ones shy away from the process (often, the larger kids). Though it may be tempting to allow reluctant students not to try, encourage their participation. Often these young people find easy excuses to quit, and this exercise may help them push through challenges in other areas of their lives.

Also, as inviting as it is to offer advice for completing the task, don't do it. It's better to have the group fail miserably than accomplish something without risking its own ideas. Praise teamwork, but watch individual encouragement. It's easy to praise athletic ability while overlooking the tremendous achievement of those who wouldn't normally attempt such a feat.

After seven minutes, ask:

● **How did you feel when you first saw the rope and heard the challenge?** (*I was afraid we couldn't do it; confident.*)

● **What emotion did you experience when the first person successfully crossed over?** (*Confidence; concern; worry.*)

● **What was the most difficult part of getting over the rope? Explain.** *(Getting the first or last people over; trusting others to catch me.)*

● **What part was easiest? Explain.**

● **Did any of you really not want to go over the rope? Explain.** *(I was embarrassed; I'm afraid of heights.)*

● **How did you feel when you successfully completed the rope exercise?** *(Proud; confident.)*

● **In what ways did you fail in this exercise?** *(I couldn't get over the rope; we couldn't decide on a plan.)*

● **Is there anything you'd do differently if you could do it again? Explain.**

● **How is this exercise like facing problems or trials in life?** *(I'm sometimes too afraid to succeed; I like the challenge of overcoming problems.)*

Have someone read aloud James 1:1-12.

Ask:

● **What does this passage say about facing trials?** *(It's good to face tough times; we can handle tough times.)*

Say: **Usually our reaction to problems dictates the outcome. If we cling to problems, we miss possibilities. If we fear obstacles, we overlook opportunities. We can learn from a famous biblical character how to approach life's tests.**

Form five groups (a group may be one or more people). Write each of the following Scripture references and summary words on an index card:

● Genesis 37:1-4 (Hate)
● Genesis 37:5-11 (Jealousy)
● Genesis 37:18-28 (Slave)
● Genesis 39:6-23 (Imprisoned)
● Genesis 40:1-23 (Forgotten)

Give each group an index card and a Bible. Tell them to read the passage and then create a wordless image of the word using all the members of their group. For example, students with the word "Hate" might simply stand in a circle, with fists raised and faces plastered with angry looks. Allow groups five minutes to read their Scriptures and create an image.

Beginning with the Genesis 37:1-4 group, have groups each present their wordless image and challenge the rest of the class to guess the word in a minute or less. After the class guesses the word or a minute has elapsed, a group spokesperson should briefly tell about the group's Scripture. After all the teams have presented their images, have them gather back in their groups and answer the following question: **When have you experienced a state like this?**

Say: **We've learned in our study that Joseph experienced some pretty rough times in his life. However, Joseph's faith in God kept him strong through it all. In the end, his problems produced possibilities—as the right-hand man for Pharaoh!**

Everyday Celebrations

Purpose:

Students will learn that the Bible gives a lot of reasons to celebrate.

Supplies:

You'll need Bibles, paper, pencils, and common household items such as hammers, cooking utensils, socks, school-books, and cans of food. You'll also need enough photocopies of the "Good Time" handout (p. 58) so each group of four can have one.

Experience:

Form groups of four or fewer. Give each group paper, pencils, and one common household item.

Say: **Each item has one obvious purpose. Take a couple minutes to determine as many alternative uses as you can for your item. List these on your paper. Don't list only the obvious. Be creative. In a few minutes, we'll see which group is able to come up with the most ideas.**

After two or three minutes, determine which group had the most ideas. Have everyone cheer for that group. Then allow groups to share several of their ideas. Then say: **These items can all serve one other purpose. They can be everyday reminders that God gives us a reason to celebrate. Take a moment to think about the item your group has. Think of one way your item reminds you of how God works in your life. Then tell us why that's worth celebrating.**

For instance, suppose the item is an eraser. You could say, "This eraser reminds me of God's forgiveness. It erases mistakes like God's forgiveness erases my sins. It's worth celebrating because God's forgiveness makes it possible for me to live eternally."

Allow the groups a few minutes to work on their ideas. Then have groups share their thoughts about their items. Praise their efforts, and acknowledge that some items will be tougher to deal with than others.

After all the groups have spoken, ask:

● **How was the exercise like trying to find reasons to celebrate your life as a Christian?** *(Sometimes it's not easy, other times it is; some people find it easier to have fun or celebrate their Christian life than others.)*

● **How do you react toward people who seem to have obvious reasons to celebrate what God has given them, but never do?** *(I get frustrated with them; angry at them; I feel like they really don't deserve everything they have.)*

● **How do you feel about people who seem to have every reason to be angry at God, but can still celebrate life?** *(Respectful; God should visibly bless them more.)*

● **You've come up with some great reasons to celebrate. Why do you think so many people who aren't Christians have the idea that Christians can't have any fun?** *(Even though Christians have reasons to celebrate, they don't always; sometimes Christians' attitudes are pretty sour; sometimes they don't know Christians well enough.)*

Say: **Regardless of what other people think, the Bible gives a lot of reasons to celebrate and many examples of celebration.**

Give each group a photocopy of the "Good Time" handout (p. 58), a Bible, and a pencil. Instruct groups each to read their passage aloud and then work together to fill out their handout. Give them five to eight minutes to complete the handout.

After the groups are done, allow them to share a few of their discoveries with the whole group.

Then ask:

● **Why did God create so many reasons for celebration?** *(He wanted us to enjoy life; he wanted to express his love for us.)*

● **What are some inappropriate ways people celebrate?** *(By using drugs or alcohol; by destroying other people's property; by attending concerts or parties that don't show respect for God.)*

● **What are some ways to have fun without compromising your faith?** *(Nonalcoholic parties; church activities; Christian concerts; amusement parks.)*

Say: **The next time your non-Christian friends say "Christians are boring," remember this activity and that Christians have lots of reasons to celebrate.**

A Good Time

Read the following verses of Scripture: Luke 15:1-32; James 1:17-18; and Revelation 19:1-9. Then using the Scriptures as a reference, "pack" reasons God has given us to celebrate in the "party van" below. After you've packed the reasons from the Scriptures, add some more of your own reasons to celebrate.

New birth through the word of truth: James 1:18

The Fruit Solution

Purpose:

Students will learn that through Jesus we can have a peaceful relationship with God that we couldn't have any other way.

Supplies:

You'll need enough photocopies of the "Battle of Appearna" handouts (p. 61) so each person can have either the Country A or Country B section of the handout. You'll also need paper and pencils.

Experience:

Form two groups. Have one group go to another room or at least go as far away as possible within your room. Give each person in one group the Country A section of the "Battle of Appearna" handout (p. 61). Give students in the other group the Country B section. Tell groups they have five minutes to read their handouts and come up with their plans.

After five minutes, bring the groups together, and let Country A present its plan. Then let students from Country B say what they don't like about the plan. Let Country B present its plan, and let students from Country A say what they don't like about it.

When both groups have reported and responded, ask:

● **What is the problem with both of these plans?** *(They hurt people; they don't make everyone happy.)*

● **Do you think there's any way to make everyone happy in this situation?** *(No way; someone's got to lose.)*

Say: **I think we may be missing something. Let me read the instructions given to each team.**

Read aloud both sets of instructions. Then say: **I think I have a solution. See what you think of it. Country A wants the appearna fruit for its seeds. Country B wants the fruit for everything but its seeds. Country A will send workers to Country B to cut the seeds out of the fruit. Then Country B will allow Country A to have the seeds free of charge to make medicine, and Country B will have the fruit to feed to its animals.**

Say: **Both countries wanted the same thing, but someone else had** to provide a solution to make them both happy.

Ask:

● **What was it like to discover there was a solution that could make you both happy? Explain.** *(I didn't like killing everyone; I felt cheated—I wanted a big war.)*

● **How was my providing a solution like what Jesus did for us when he died on the cross?** *(God wanted us to have peace with him, and we wanted peace, too, but no one else could provide it; Jesus gave us the solution to our conflict.)*

Say: **Through Jesus we can have a peaceful relationship with God that we couldn't have any other way. And because he's done that for us, we need to live our lives in thankfulness to him.**

Form groups of three or four, and give each person a sheet of paper and a pencil.

Say to the groups: **Someone you know at school claims to be an atheist, but lately he's been talking to you about who Jesus is. Using Colossians 1:15-23, work with your group members to put together a description of who Jesus is and what he has done. Then write one sentence telling your friend why you believe in Jesus.**

Give groups about ten minutes, then have them report what they wrote. Ask:

● **Thinking about all the things you wrote in your descriptions of Jesus, how do those descriptions make you feel about Jesus?** *(Grateful; loving; thankful.)*

● **How do those things make you feel about your atheist friend? Explain.** *(Sad that he doesn't know the truth; wishing I could convince her of the truth.)*

● **If a person you know today did something to save you from certain death and crippled himself doing it, how would you act toward that person from now on?** *(I'd be his servant; I'd do things to please him.)*

Say: **Jesus has done so much for us. And we should do everything we can to express our thankfulness to him.**

Battle of Appearna

Cut apart the following directions for your groups.

Country A

Your country desperately needs appearna fruit. You've found that the seeds from the fruit can be dried, ground up, and used to effectively combat a disease that's killing your country's livestock. The trouble is that appearna fruit grows in only one country, and that country wants to keep all its appearna fruit for its own use. Your goal is to think of a way—whatever it takes—to get that appearna fruit for your country.

Country B

Your country is the only country in the world that can grow appearna fruit. You use the fruit to feed your livestock because normal grain won't grow in your country. But you have to cut the seeds out of the fruit because they make the animals sick. Another country wants your appearna fruit. Your goal is to devise a way to protect your fruit no matter what the other country does to try to get it.

Hidden Gifts

Purpose:

Teenagers will explore how the Holy Spirit empowers each of us to minister to others through specific gifts and abilities.

Supplies:

You'll need Bibles, candy, pencils, and one photocopy of the "Gifts of the Holy Spirit" handout (p. 64) for each group of four.

Experience:

Before this activity, hide one piece of candy (choose different kinds or flavors so kids won't find the same kind) for each group member somewhere in the room.

Say: **Remember when you were younger and searched for candy on Easter morning? Well today we're going to regress a bit and participate in a similar kind of candy hunt. I've hidden one piece of candy for each person somewhere in this room. When I say "go," your job is to find one piece of candy and then sit down. Once you've found your candy, you may not help anyone else look for a piece of candy. We'll play until every person has found one piece of candy.**

Play for five minutes or so, or until each student has found a piece of candy. If some students are still looking after five minutes, call time, and have kids form a circle.

Ask:

● **What went through your mind when you found a piece of candy?** *(I was disappointed; I wanted to help someone else; I was happy.)*

● **How is this like the way people feel when they discover an ability or talent they have? How is it different? Explain.** *(It's similar, people feel good when they realize they're good at something; it's different, talents come from within and the candy was a gift.)*

● **What was it like to search for your candy?** *(It was easy; it was frustrating.)*

● **How is that like the way people discover their spiritual gifts?** *(People don't always find their gifts; some people know right away what their gifts are, others don't ever know.)*

Distribute a piece of candy to anyone who didn't find one. Have students eat their candy.

Say: **Not everyone had the same flavor of candy. Likewise, we don't all have the same spiritual gifts. The Bible gives us insight into the gifts of the Holy Spirit and what they mean for us. Let's explore what the Bible has to say.**

Form groups of no more than four. Give groups each a "Gifts of the Holy Spirit" handout (p. 64), a Bible, and a pencil. Say: **Read the Bible passages listed on the handout. Work together in your group to find and list the spiritual gifts described in those passages in the space provided. Then talk about what those gifts mean, and write a definition for each on your handout.**

After about five minutes, call time. Have groups each tell what they found and define one or two of the spiritual gifts they listed. Check out the "Gifts" box for a listing of spiritual gifts students might come up with.

Ask:

● **What surprised you most about the spiritual gifts you found?** *(There were more than I thought; I don't know what all of them mean; some are pretty common.)*

● **Was it easy to define the gifts? Why or why not?** *(Yes, most were pretty obvious; no, some didn't make sense to me.)*

Read aloud 1 Corinthians 12:12-18.

Ask:

● **What does this passage tell us about the gifts of the Spirit?** *(Each is important; God has chosen each person's gifts for a purpose.)*

Say: **The Holy Spirit empowers each of us to minister to others through specific gifts and abilities. Since the Holy Spirit is our "helper," these gifts are "helps" for us to better serve and worship God in the world around us.**

This is a good opportunity to incorporate your church's beliefs about the gifts of the Spirit. You may want to have a pastor visit the class to briefly discuss how you interpret the Bible passages describing spiritual gifts. Some questions you might want to have the pastor answer might include:

● What spiritual gifts do we acknowledge in our church?

● What is the role of each gift?

● What kind of emphasis do we place on the gifts of the Spirit?

Gifts

Administration—Providing organization and coordination within the church.

Apostleship—Unique call and commission by Jesus.

Discernment—Understanding the spiritual source behind specific actions.

Encouragement—Building others up.

Evangelism—Telling others about Christ.

Faith—Believing in God's power to do the impossible.

Giving—Being generous and giving money or gifts to God's work.

Healing—Healing spiritual, emotional, and physical pain.

Helping—Ministering to the practical needs of others.

Interpretation of Tongues—Translating a message from someone speaking in tongues.

Leadership—Motivating and directing others in ministry.

Mercy—Ministering to those who suffer.

Miracles—Supernatural demonstration of God's power.

Prophecy—Presenting messages from God about present or future situations.

Serving—Ministering to others through practical service.

Shepherding—Pastoring and nurturing other Christians.

Teaching—Communicating the truths of Scripture to others.

Tongues—Praising God in a foreign or "prayer" language.

Word of Knowledge—Knowing truths about another person or situation.

Gifts of the Holy Spirit

Look up the following passages, and list gifts of the Holy Spirit in the "Gifts of the Holy Spirit" column of the chart below. Then discuss what each gift means, and write a short definition in the "What the Gifts Mean" column.

- Romans 12:3-8

- 1 Corinthians 12:4-11

- 1 Corinthians 12:28

- Ephesians 4:7-12

Gifts of the Holy Spirit	What the Gifts Mean

The Hunt

Purpose:

Teenagers will explore how God's Word lights our paths.

Supplies:

You'll need Bibles, paper, pencils, a desk lamp, a treasure (such as a couple of bags of gold-coin candy or other items kids can share), and one copy of the "Treasure Instructions" handout (p. 67).

Experience:

Before class, carefully hide the treasure somewhere in or near your meeting room. Be sure it's not too easy to find.

Photocopy the "Treasure Instructions" handout (p. 67), and title another piece of paper "Treasure Map." On the "Treasure Map," write at the top, "Follow the map to find the hidden treasure." Then draw a simple map showing precisely where the treasure is, and describe it. Don't write or draw anything on the "Treasure Instructions" handout. Fold both papers in half.

Form two teams. Tell kids they're going on a treasure hunt. Say: **The team that finds the treasure first gets to keep it. Your instructions are secret. Don't let the other team see your instructions.**

Give one team the "Treasure Map" and the other team the "Treasure Instructions" handout. Have teams each look for the treasure.

The team with the map should find the treasure quickly. The other team may quickly complain about the unfairness of the hunt. Let the complaining go on for a bit; then bring the group together for discussion.

Ask:

● **Why was it so easy for one group to find the treasure?** *(They had a map; they knew what the treasure was.)*

● **What did the map and the description do for the winning group?** *(It helped them know what they were looking for; they knew exactly where to look.)*

● **How is the treasure map in this activity like the Bible in our lives?** *(They both help us find our way; they both help us know what to look for.)*

Say: **The Bible is kind of like a treasure map; it's a handbook to help us find and build a relationship with God. Now let's look at what God says about how we're to use the Bible.**

Give the losing team a "good sport" treasure—one just like the winning team's treasure.

Plug in and turn on the desk lamp you brought to class. Then ask one of your students to sit by the desk lamp and read aloud Psalm 119:102-108. As the person begins reading, turn off the other lights in the room and darken the room as much as possible. As soon as the student completes verse 105, turn off the lamp. The student may be able to finish reading, depending on how dark the room is.

When the student is finished or stops, ask:

● **What did the lamp do for the person reading?** *(It gave him light; it helped her see the words.)*

● **In this passage, the psalmist is comparing God's Word to a lamp. How is the Bible like a lamp for us?** *(It helps us see where we're going; it helps us see where we are.)*

Say: **God has given us the Bible to help us find our way—like a lamp in the darkness. Now let's see just how it does that.**

Form pairs, and give each pair a sheet of paper, a pencil, and a Bible. Say: **Each pair is a team of doctors. Your patient is the person described in 2 Timothy 3:17, but that patient isn't well—not able to do "every good work." Your job is to prescribe the medicine the patient needs to survive. You'll find that medicine in 2 Timothy 3:16.**

Have pairs each write their recommendations.

Ask:

● **What's your recommended prescription?** *(Teaching; learning what's wrong; learning how to live right.)*

● **How can these prescriptions help us?** *(They help us see when we do wrong; they tell us what we need to know to do what's right.)*

● **How would trying to live for God without the Bible be like walking down an unfamiliar path in the dark?** *(Both would be very tough; I'd stumble a lot either way.)*

Say: **God's Word lights our paths. It helps us find our way, but only if we let it.**

Have partners congratulate each other on a good diagnosis by gently patting each other on the back as they speak.

Treasure Instructions

Look around the area to find a treasure.

Incommunicado

Purpose:

Teenagers will discover how to build their relationship with God through the study of his Word.

Supplies:

You'll need Bibles, one photocopy of the "Personal Bible Discovery" handout (p. 70), and a pencil for each person.

Experience:

Have students each pair up with the person in the room they know the least. Then say: **Sit down with your partner for two minutes to learn more about each other. There's only one catch: You can't talk to each other, write notes, touch each other, or use any other communication. You must simply sit near each other.**

After two minutes of awkward silence and giggles, ask:

● **How much did you learn?** *(Not much, since we couldn't talk; nothing, we needed to communicate.)*

● **Is it possible to develop a relationship with someone without communication?** *(No, you can't develop a relationship without learning about someone; no, you've got to be able to talk.)*

● **Think about your relationship with the parent you're closest to. How would that relationship develop if you couldn't communicate in any way?** *(It would be tough; we'd grow farther apart.)*

● **How is trying to learn about each other without communicating like trying to develop a relationship with God without reading the Bible?** *(You can't get to know God without taking in his Word; it's similar, but you can get to know God in other ways, too.)*

● **To develop a close relationship with God, what do we need to do?** *(Study the Bible; pray.)*

Say: **God reveals himself to us through his Word. And to develop our relationship with God, we need to take in his Word by reading it. Let's look at how a few Bible characters worked on their relationships with God.**

Give each person a Bible, a pencil, and a "Personal Bible Discovery" handout (p. 70). Form three groups. If you have more than fifteen kids, form more groups so no group has more than five people. Assign one of these passages to each group:

- Abram (Genesis 12:1-4)
- Daniel (Daniel 6:6-11)
- Jesus (Matthew 14:13-14, 23)

Have groups each use the handout to work through their passage. When groups are finished, have them each report their findings.

Then ask:

● **What have we learned from this study?** *(How Bible characters worked on their relationship with God; how important it is to spend time alone with God; how we can get more out of personal Bible study.)*

Students' answers to the question will vary, but be sure to direct them to come up with all of the above answers.

Say: **If it was important for Jesus to stay in contact with God, then think how important it must be for us, too. As we stay in touch with God through his Word, our relationship with him will grow.**

Personal Bible Discovery

Use the four questions on this sheet to help you study your assigned passage.
Then keep the questions to help you in your own personal Bible study.

PASSAGE

WHAT'S IT SAY?

(In a nutshell, what's the message of this passage?)

WHAT'S IT MEAN?

(What does this passage suggest people should do to respond?)

WHAT'S IT MEAN TO ME?

(How does this passage apply to me?)

WHAT AM I GOING TO DO ABOUT IT?

(What will I do in response to the message of this passage?)

Island of Whadyado

Purpose:

Students will discover that the heart of all true worship is love for God.

Supplies:

You'll need Bibles, one photocopy of the "Worship on Whadyado" handout (p. 73) for each group of four, one photocopy of the "Worship: Group Assignments" worksheet (p. 74), pencils, newsprint, markers, and tape.

Experience:

Form groups of no more than four.

Say: **Pretend we're the first Christian missionaries to a small island called Whadyado. These people have a very different culture than any we've encountered before.**

Our first responsibility as missionaries is to design a worship program for these people. Remember—these people are not like us, and their style of worship will need to be different from ours.

Provide each group with a pencil and a photocopy of the "Worship on Whadyado" handout (p. 73). Allow ten minutes for students to work on this assignment.

When everyone is ready, have each group act out the worship program they designed for the people of Whadyado.

After the presentations, congratulate students on their creativity. Then ask:

● **What are your thoughts about what we just did?** *(I felt pretty stupid; I felt uncomfortable.)*

● **Was the assignment difficult for you? Why or why not?** *(Yes, I didn't have enough information; yes, I didn't know enough about what the Bible says about worship.)*

● **Did we worship together as a group just now? Explain.** *(Yes, we were being sincere; no, we were each doing our own thing.)*

● **What would have to change for us to worship "together"?** *(We'd* *all have to agree on what we should do; we'd have to have the right attitude.)*

● **Which do you think is more important: the method of worship or the attitude of worship? Explain.** *(The attitude, because God looks at the heart; the method and the attitude are equally important because we need to be unified in our worship.)*

Say: **Many churches differ in their method of worship. And that's OK. But the Corinthian Christians had the wrong attitude in their worship, and that made their actions wrong. Let's look more closely at why Paul confronted them.**

Form two groups. Give each group a photocopy of one of the assignments on the "Worship: Group Assignments" handout (p. 74). If you have time, allow students to lead the class in their worship time. If there isn't enough time for students to lead a worship time, ask them to share their plans for worship.

Write "Love" in large letters across the top of a sheet of newsprint, and tape it to the wall. Read aloud 1 Corinthians 13. Ask:

● **What part does love play in worship?** *(Without love, worship is meaningless; love is the reason we worship.)*

Assign each person one verse from 1 Corinthians 13. It's OK if more than one person is assigned the same verse. Tell students each to write on the newsprint a description of love found in their verse. When everyone is finished, read all the descriptions and congratulate students on their efforts.

Say: **These are wonderful truths about love. And they all share one thing in common—they're all active. Love is almost always something you do, not just something you feel. Let's explore how we can actively show love to God through our worship.**

Have students brainstorm about how they can be more involved in the worship experiences of their church. Ask students to tell one or two ways they'll begin to show God their love by actively worshipping him.

Say: **Worship is many things to many people. But the heart of all true worship is the same—love for God. Without love, worship is meaningless.**

Worship on Whadyado

Use these guidelines to help you develop a worship program for natives on the island of Whadyado.

1. The islanders love to move around.

2. The islanders believe running is a high form of praise to their old pagan gods.

3. The islanders have a high value for physical touch.

4. The islanders are afraid of loud voices.

5. The islanders have a high value for quiet contemplation.

6. The islanders love to drum.

7. The islanders greet one another by rubbing their ears against their neighbors'.

8. The islanders never pray without first grabbing their ankles.

Worship: Group Assignments

Group 1:

Read 1 Corinthians 14:26-33a. Work together as a group to pull from the passage two or three "guiding principles" for worship according to Paul. Then design an outdoor worship service about creation based on Psalm 104. Use these questions to guide your worship experience:

1. What outdoor setting will you choose?

2. What instructions will you give the worshipers?

3. How will you lead this service?

4. Will you include songs? List them.

5. What are some truths from Psalm 104 that you might want to share?

Group 2:

Read 1 Corinthians 14:26-33a. Work together as a group to pull from the passage two or three "guiding principles" for worship according to Paul. Then design a worship experience based on the Thanksgiving holiday. Refer to Psalm 100 for ideas. Use these questions to guide your worship experience:

1. How will you set up the room?

2. What instructions will you give the worshipers?

3. How will you lead this service?

4. Will you include songs? List them.

5. What are some thanksgiving truths from Psalm 100 that you might want to share?

On the Ceiling

Purpose:

Students will explore how living the Christian life means working together as a body.

Supplies:

You'll need Bibles, tacks, tape, paper, pencils, and a poster or T-shirt displaying a Christian message for every three teenagers (or supplies for students to make their own).

Experience:

Form trios. Give each trio a poster with a Christian message on it. You can get these from the church library, a Christian bookstore, or have kids create them.

Say: **Following God with our lives means keeping our focus on Jesus. To remind us to do that, we're going to hang these Christian posters on the ceiling.**

Set out a box of tacks and a roll of tape. Say: **You will have thirty seconds to get your poster securely hung from the ceiling. You may use these supplies, but you may not use any props other than your bodies to reach the ceiling. On your mark, get set, go!**

Don't offer any suggestions or help. If students have difficulty with the task, allow them to be frustrated.

Call time after thirty seconds. Congratulate students who completed the task. Ask:

● **What initial reactions did you have about this assignment?** *(It seemed silly; it took a lot of teamwork.)*

● **How could anyone accomplish this goal?** *(By working together.)*

● **How is attempting to hang your poster on the ceiling like living the Christian life?** *(You need other people to help you reach your goal.)*

Say: **None of you could hang your poster unless you worked together. In the same way, living the Christian life means working together as a body. Sometimes it even means sacrificing our own wants and desires for the sake of meeting others' needs.**

Ask each person to share one positive way another person in the group helps to meet his or her needs. The help might be as simple as offering a smile or saying something encouraging.

Say: **Just like the Apostle Paul, we're each called to live for Christ by helping and encouraging each other. As we can see here, sometimes that can happen in simple, quiet ways. Let's look now at other ways we are "sent" like the apostles.**

Form three groups. Ask the first group to read 2 Corinthians 3:4-18, and determine how the new covenant is different from the old covenant. Have them develop a short skit that shows the difference between the two covenants.

Have the second group read 2 Corinthians 4:1-7. Ask them to find characteristics of the ministry of Christ. Provide pencils and paper, and instruct them to write a job description about what's required for the average person to live out the ministry of Christ.

Instruct the third group to read 2 Corinthians 4:8-18. Tell them to look at these contrasts of ministry:

- troubles all around but not defeated,
- don't know what to do but don't give up the hope of living,
- persecuted but God stays constant, and
- hurt but not destroyed.

Ask them to tell a story about a hero, true or fictional, that illustrates each contrast.

Allow several minutes for preparation. Then have each group present and explain its work. Congratulate students' efforts; then ask:

- **Why is it important for all of us to be involved in the ministry of Christ?** *(Because people need to learn about Jesus; because Jesus asked all of his followers to be involved.)*

- **What is hard for you personally about being involved in Christ's ministry?** *(It's hard for me to reach out to others; it's hard for me to find time.)*

Say: **No one ever said that living for Jesus would be easy. But as Christians, God "sends" each of us out into the world to bring Christ's love and grace to those who need it.**

Orders From the King

Purpose:

Teenagers will learn from Mary's story why it's important to be willing to do whatever God asks, no matter how difficult.

Supplies:

You'll need one photocopy of the "Royal Demands and Servant Actions" handout (p. 79) for each pair. You'll also need Bibles, paper, and pencils.

Experience:

Form pairs. Have each pair separate from other pairs as much as possible. In each pair, designate one "king" or "queen" and one "servant." Cut apart the two sections of the "Royal Demands and Servant Actions" handouts (p. 79), and give the king or queen in each pair the "Royal Demands" section. Give the servant partner a copy of the "Servant Actions" section. Have the kings and queens start giving demands, and have the servants follow their instructions. Wander around to be sure kings and queens aren't giving commands not listed on their sheets.

After about three minutes, bring the group together, and ask:

● **What was it like being a king or queen?** *(I felt great; I felt powerful; I didn't want to be a leader.)*

● **What was it like being a servant?** *(I hated it; I felt dirty.)*

● **What was your attitude toward your king or queen?** *(I despised him; I decided it was my job to please her.)*

● **Does God want us to be more like the kings and queens or the servants? Explain.** *(The servants, he wants us to serve him; the kings and queens, he wants us to live abundant lives.)*

● **How are God's commands different from our kings' and queens' commands?** *(He wants us to do things good for us, not just for him; his commands aren't so mean.)*

● **How should our attitudes as servants of God be different from the attitudes of our servants today?** *(We should be happy to serve God; we* *should be more willing to do what he wants.)*

Say: **Today we're going to talk about a particular servant of God who is a biblical heroine because she was willing to do something very difficult. We're going to study Mary, the mother of Jesus.**

First, I want to ask the girls a question. What would your parents say if you came to them and said you had never had sex but you were pregnant; furthermore, an angel had told you in a dream that the baby was to be the Son of God?

After a couple of minutes for laughs and horror stories, say: **That's not far from what Mary had to do. Let's read the story.**

Hand out Bibles, and have students turn to Luke 1:26-38. Ask volunteers to read the passage aloud, taking turns reading two verses at a time.

When students have finished the reading, ask:

● **What kind of person do you think God would have chosen to be the mother of Jesus?** *(A faithful, obedient woman; someone who would take good care of Jesus.)*

● **How do you think Mary felt when she found out what God wanted her to do?** *(Honored; frightened; worried.)*

● **What kinds of responses might you have given in Mary's situation?** *(Couldn't you find somebody better? What will my parents say?)*

● **What was Mary's response in the end?** *(I'm willing; OK, Lord.)*

● **How was Mary's response like or unlike the responses of our servants a few minutes ago?** *(It was like our responses because she did what God wanted, the way the servants did; it was different because she willingly did it and our servants didn't want to follow the demands.)*

Say: **Mary is a heroine to us because she gave us an example of an incredible willingness to do whatever God asked of her.**

Form groups of three or four. Give each group paper and a pencil, and say: **Talk among your group, and decide on what might be the three toughest things God might want you to do with your life.**

Give students a couple of minutes to create their lists. Then say: **Now decide on what might be the three toughest things God might want you to do this week.**

After a couple more minutes say: **Now think about those six things as I read this verse.**

Read aloud Philippians 4:19. Then read it one more time.

Say: **God promises to meet all our needs when we're following him. Think about what commitment you want to make to him related to those six tough things your group came up with. He might not ever want you to be a missionary in Morocco, but he wants you to be willing to do whatever he asks of you—the way Mary was willing.**

Give students a minute of silence to think and pray. Then have students each tell the person on their right ways that person can serve God.

Royal Demands and Servant Actions

Royal Demands

Choose any commands from the list below, and demand that your servant do them.

Tie my shoes.

Give me a shoulder and neck rub.

Shine my shoes.

Sit down on the floor at my feet.

Kneel and bow facing me.

Shine my fingernails.

Take off my shoes and scratch my feet.

Read to me.

Servant Actions

Do whatever your king or queen tells
you to do without griping or complaining.

Outdo Each Other

Purpose:

Teenagers will discover that serving others can be fun.

Supplies:

You'll need Bibles, masking tape, pencils, paper, and one copy of the "Outdo Each Other" handout (p. 82) for each group member.

Experience:

Give each group member an "Outdo Each Other" handout (p. 82), a piece of masking tape, and a pencil. Instruct the students to tape the handout onto each other's backs.

Say: **We're going to have a contest in service. Each of you has a list of services on your backs that you need to have done for you. The idea is to outdo others in the class by doing the service items listed on their backs before all the items on your list are completed. When you do a service for someone else, sign the appropriate area on his or her handout. No one may refuse to be served, and you may only sign off one item per list.**

If your list gets filled with names, move it to your front and continue to work at filling out others' lists. The last person with a list on his or her back is the winner. Ready? Go serve!

When the game is finished, ask:

● **What thoughts did you have as you served the people around you during the contest?** *(I enjoyed it; it was frantic; I didn't know what to think.)*

● **What was it like to have others serve you? Explain.** *(Strange, I was losing ground in the contest if they served me; great, it was set up so everyone won by serving.)*

● **How would you describe the atmosphere in the classroom while you were all trying to outdo one another in serving?** *(Crazy; hectic; fun; friendly.)*

● **What would life be like if all Christians had an attitude about serving like the one that was needed to win this contest?** *(People would have a lot of friends; people would probably be happier; people might think Christians were really weird; Christians might think Christians were a lot of fun.)*

Say: **As you just found out, attitude has a lot to do with how much someone enjoys serving. Serving can be fun, if you want it to be. That's not to say serving isn't serious stuff, but it's not all boring stuff either.**

Have students form groups of six or fewer, and give groups each a Bible, a sheet of paper, and a pencil. Instruct each group to read Luke 10:1-2, 17 and Ephesians 6:7-8 aloud. Then advise the groups to create a skit, rap, song, or cheer that reflects the Scripture passages they read. Encourage groups to be creative and to have fun. Make sure to point out that each group member must participate in the final product.

After a few minutes, allow the groups to perform their dramatics. Then ask:

● **How do you think the seventy-two followers felt when Jesus first sent them out?** *(Nervous; fun; excited; scared; stupid.)*

● **How do you think they felt when they came back?** *(Thrilled; happy; joyful; sad it was over; powerful.)*

● **Are their experiences like our lives today? How?** *(Jesus wants us to go out serving others, too; sometimes we feel unsure about following Jesus' instructions; God will empower us to complete the tasks he has for us.)*

Reread Ephesians 6:7-8 aloud for the class.

Ask:

● **How would you say this passage in your own words?**

● **What are everyday opportunities we have to serve wholeheartedly?** *(Clean our room; help our parents with chores; help our friends with schoolwork; run errands for the neighbors; tell others about Jesus.)*

Say: **Few things are more exciting than making an impact on those around us. Sometimes that calls for a risk on our part. Are we willing to risk being a servant? Jesus risked it all when he served us by dying on the cross. But the reward was that we all got the opportunity to become friends with God again. That reward means eternal joy for both us and Jesus.**

Outdo Each Other

Try to do as many of the items below for others in the group before they do them all for you. Sign the space next to the items you do on each person's sheet.

- I have no hands. Will you comb my hair? _____
- I have no hands. Will you scratch my nose? _____
- I'm lost. Will you help me find my chair? _____
- I haven't learned how yet. Will you tie my shoes?

  _____

- I'm feeling a little sick. Will you draw me a map to the

  restroom? _____
  - I'm color blind. Please help me find someone with red on. _____
  - I'm so thirsty. Will you draw me a map to the water fountain? _____

- I forgot my Bible. Will you get me one I can use? _____
- I'm blind. Will you lead me over to sit on a chair?

  _____

- I have no hands. Will you take my shoes off for me?

  _____

- I'm new. Will you introduce me to the leader? _____
  - I'm so sad. Will you help me get hugs from three people? _____
  - I have no hands. Will you scratch my back?

  _____

The Pain

Purpose:

Teenagers will examine the pain Jesus felt on the cross and discover why Jesus' death on the cross was God's great act of forgiveness.

Supplies:

You'll need Bibles, pencils, tape, markers, candles, matches, and one copy of the "My Life" (p. 85) and "At the Cross" handouts (p. 86) for each person.

Experience:

This lesson includes activities that may make your class feel uncomfortable. Be prepared for students' responses to the lesson. Some may giggle or laugh to release tension, others may cry during one of the activities. Be sure to talk about how students are feeling throughout the lesson.

This may be an appropriate lesson to share the message of Christ with non-Christians in your class.

Give each person a "My Life" handout (p. 85) and a pencil. Have students complete the handouts.

Afterward, have students tape the handouts to the wall. Give each teenager a marker.

Say: **These papers represent who you are. For this next activity, we'll imagine these papers are you.**

On "go," use the markers to deface your own handout. You may write derogatory names such as "Bible baby" or "Holy roller" on the sheets, but don't use profanity. You may even tear the papers if you want. When I call time, stop defacing the papers and step back from the wall.

Give students a minute or two to deface the handouts. Then call time. Have students collect their papers and sit in a circle.

Ask:

● **What reactions do you have as you look at your paper?** *(I feel sad; it doesn't affect me; I'm upset.)*

● **How is that like the way God feels when he sees our sins?** *(He's sad; it makes God angry.)*

● **What went through your mind as you defaced your paper?** *(It felt uncomfortable; I enjoyed it; nothing.)*

● **In what ways do we sometimes deface Jesus' name?** *(By lying; by not spending enough time in prayer; by swearing.)*

● **Who were the people who "defaced" Jesus at the time of his crucifixion?** *(The Roman soldiers; the Jews; everyone.)*

● **Look at your paper. How does the way it looks reflect what sin does to our lives?** *(Sin tears us apart; sin hurts us; we all sin.)*

Say: **Just as we may have felt bad about the ruined papers, God must feel bad about the sin in people's lives. He wanted to reconcile the world to himself, so he sent Jesus to die for our sins. Though we deserved to die, Jesus died in our place. Jesus' agony on the cross was probably much more than physical pain. He knew he shouldered the sins of the world as he hung from the cross.**

Place five candles in a circle. Light them and turn out the lights. Give each person an "At the Cross" handout (p. 86). Say: **This handout contains a short reader's theater play based on Jesus' crucifixion. Follow the instructions, and read together when your part comes up. Remember to make this a serious time—imagine you're actually at Jesus' crucifixion as you read your part.**

Read the narrator's part and have students follow along, reading the guys' or girls' parts as appropriate. Students will have to stay close to the candles to read their scripts. As the script is read, blow out one candle every time you see a small candle on the script. Just after students read the last section, blow out the final candle and remain silent for a moment.

Then turn on the lights, and have someone read aloud Matthew 27:32-56. Ask:

● **What thoughts did you have as you read the script?** *(I was uncomfortable; I felt sad; it made me angry.)*

● **What do the play and the Scripture passage tell us about Jesus' death on the cross?** *(It was a powerful event; it was a painful time for Jesus.)*

● **How might Jesus' death be a stumbling block for some people?** *(They wonder why he had to die; they don't believe he rose again.)*

● **How might Jesus' death be a source of power for people?** *(His death allows us to reach God; by his death we're freed from sin.)*

● **Why is Jesus' death on the cross important?** *(Because only God's Son could die for our sins; if he didn't die, our sins wouldn't be forgiven; since he didn't have any sins, his death took away our sins.)*

Say: **Jesus' death on the cross was God's great act of forgiveness. And that message of forgiveness should remind us to follow in Jesus' example and forgive others as he forgave us.**

My Life

Think of this handout as a picture of you. Complete the sections below to describe your life.

Name:

Complete the following sentences.

- Three unique things about me are…

- If I could do anything I wanted, I'd…

- If I were to describe myself to a stranger, I'd say…

- My life is…

Draw a self-portrait below.

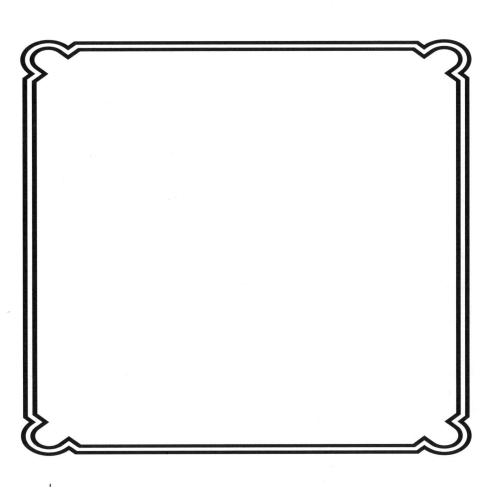

At the Cross

There are three different parts in this drama: Narrator,
Guys, and Girls. Read aloud your part in turn.

Narrator: At noon, the whole country was covered with darkness. The people watched as Jesus hung on the cross. Some were there out of curiosity. Some came to cry for him. Others came to mock him. Out of the darkness, Jesus cried aloud from the cross, "My God, my God, why have you forsaken me?"

Guys: What'd he say?

Girls: He's crying out for his God.

Narrator: People nearby tried to make Jesus drink some cheap wine. They took a sponge, soaked it in the wine, then held it out on a long stick to Jesus' lips.

Guys: Here, drink it. Drink it! It'll ease the pain.

Girls: Wait, let him suffer! Let's see if Elijah is coming to save him now.

Narrator: *(A loud cry of Jesus' dying breath)* "Ahhhhhh!" *(Pause.)* With one final cry, Jesus gave up his spirit. Suddenly the earth shook. Graves opened and people who were buried came to life. Everywhere, people scattered in panic.

Girls: What's that? What's happening?

Guys: *(Frightened)* It's an earthquake! Run!

Girls: What does this mean?

Guys: It's him! It's all because of Jesus.

Girls: It can't be. He's just a man...or could he be...?

Guys: The Son of God?

All: He was the Son of God. Oh, how I wish I'd followed him.

Narrator: As evening came, Joseph of Arimathea took Jesus to a tomb and buried him.

Perfect Score

Purpose:

Students will learn from Peter's story how imperfect people can be used in mighty ways by God.

Supplies:

You'll need Bibles, paper, pencils, small prizes such as candy bars, and two copies of the "Hero Hall of Fame Induction Evaluation" (p. 89).

Experience:

Say: **We're going to play a little Bible trivia game. You're not competing against each other. You're competing to see how many answers you can get right. Everyone getting an acceptable number right will get a prize.**

Give each student paper and a pencil; then read the following questions. Have enough small prizes, such as candy bars, ready to give to all the students.

Give students only about fifteen seconds on each question, but don't read the answers until you've read all the questions.

1. **Who wrestled with an angel?** *(Jacob)*
2. **Where did Job live?** *(Uz)*
3. **Who was the left-handed judge?** *(Ehud)*
4. **Where was Jesus anointed with perfume?** *(Bethany)*
5. **Why did Paul go to the island of Malta?** *(He was shipwrecked there.)*

When you've finished, give the answers, and ask how many got all the answers right. It's not likely that anyone will have a perfect score, but if someone does, give that person a prize.

Then say: **Only people with perfect scores get the prize. That's how things work, isn't it? You have to be perfect to be a real hero, right?**

Ask:

● **How did it feel to get wrong answers? Explain.** *(Lousy, I like to be right; not so bad, I knew I wouldn't do well.)*

● **What went through your mind when you heard that only people with perfect scores would get prizes? Explain.** *(I was angry, I only missed one; it was no big deal, I knew I wouldn't get a prize anyway.)*

● **How is this like you sometimes feel when you mess up in real**

life? *(It's different, I can do better in life; kind of the same, I make a lot of mistakes.)*

● **Do you think someone has to be perfect or close to perfect as a Christian for God to use him or her? Why or why not?** *(Yes, you have to be pretty good; no, God can use anyone.)*

Say: **Let's take a look now at someone in the Bible who made several mistakes but was still used mightily by God.**

Form two teams, and give each team a Bible, a copy of the "Hero Hall of Fame Induction Evaluation" handout (p. 89), and a pencil. Say: **You are the Hero Hall of Fame committee. You'll study the passages I give you, filling in the Hall of Fame evaluation form. Then you'll present your recommendations on the Apostle Peter. After your presentations, we'll vote on whether Peter should be inducted into the Hero Hall of Fame.**

Give the groups the following passages:

Group 1: Mark 8:27-30; Acts 2:14, 36-41.

Group 2: Matthew 14:22-31; Mark 14:27-31, 66-72.

Give groups about ten minutes to study their passages and fill out the forms. Then have them make their presentations to each other. After the presentations, pass out slips of paper and have students vote: yes, if they think Peter really is a hero; no, if they think he isn't.

Count the votes, and announce the decision. Whatever the outcome, ask:

● **Why did you vote the way you did?** *(Peter messed up; he did well in the end.)*

● **What are characteristics of a true hero?** *(Courage; honesty; humility; honor; respect.)*

● **Can a person make mistakes—even some big ones—and still become a hero? Explain.** *(Yes, if they overcome their mistakes; no, once you mess up really bad, you haven't got a chance.)*

Say: **Peter's record speaks for itself. He did mess up. But he put his mistakes behind him and became one of God's greatest leaders in the early church.**

Give the remaining prizes out to all of the students.

FORM # 189327653

Hero Hall of Fame
Induction Evaluation

Nominee's Name:

_____

_____

Nominee's Successes:

_____

_____

Nominee's Failures:

_____

_____

Examples of Nominee's Courage:

_____

_____

Examples of Nominee's Lack of Courage:

_____

_____

Committee Recommendation:

_____

_____

_____

Say What?

Purpose:

Students will learn that God has the power to meet our needs.

Supplies:

You'll need Bibles, at least one roll of pennies (double that if you have more than twenty people in your group), pencils, and one copy of the "Power to Give" handout (p. 92) for each person.

Experience:

Say: **I'd like to help each of you get enough money to buy whatever you want. So I'm going to start passing out pennies.**

Start passing out the pennies one at a time. When they're all distributed, say: **Now get up and give your pennies away. You must give all your pennies to someone else, but you may not give more than one to any one person.** After a couple minutes of confusion and trading, stop the action.

Say: **Pennies probably won't help much with your needs. So I'm going to turn each penny into a hundred-dollar bill. Ready? Here we go!** Pause for a moment. Then look at someone's pennies. Pause again; then look at the pennies. **Well, I guess I can't do it.**

When students stop jeering or laughing, say: **OK, so I didn't work a miracle. As much as I wanted to help meet your needs, I couldn't change the pennies into hundred-dollar bills. Sometimes earthly actions aren't enough to meet people's needs.**

Ask:

● **What went through your mind when I told you I wanted to help meet your needs?** *(I didn't believe you; I was intrigued.)*

● **How is that like the way people might've felt when Jesus helped meet their needs?** *(Jesus really could meet people's needs; people would've felt good about Jesus' help.)*

● **What if each penny had turned into a hundred-dollar bill?** *(We'd all be rich; we'd wonder how you did it.)*

● **Why didn't my desire to turn the pennies into hundred-dollar bills make it happen?** *(You aren't God; you can't do miracles.)*

Say: **No matter how hard we wish for something, we can't make it** happen. No matter how much I'd like to meet all your needs, I can't do it on my own.

But Jesus is different. Since he's God, he can do whatever he wants in meeting our needs. And the exciting thing is that he wants to help us!

Give each student a "Power to Give" handout (p. 92) and a pencil. Have them work individually to complete the handouts.

After students have completed their handouts, have volunteers report what they discovered. Encourage students who have different answers to speak up.

Then ask:

● **What exciting messages about Jesus can we get from these passages?** *(Jesus cares about people; Jesus can work miracles to help his people.)*

Say: **Jesus' miracles not only prove his power, but his compassion as well. And what a great combination that is! He loves us, so he wants to do things for us. And he has the power to do anything he wants. We can't lose!**

Power to Give

Read both of the passages below and then follow the instructions at the bottom.

Matthew 14:13-21

Verse 13—When Jesus heard what had happened, he withdrew by boat privately to a solitary place. Hearing of this, the crowds followed him on foot from the towns.

Verse 14—When Jesus landed and saw a large crowd, he had compassion on them and healed their sick.

Verse 15—As evening approached, the disciples came to him and said, "This is a remote place, and it's already getting late. Send the crowds away, so they can go to the villages and buy themselves some food."

Verse 16—Jesus replied, "They do not need to go away. You give them something to eat."

Verse 17—"We have here only five loaves of bread and two fish," they answered.

Verse 18—"Bring them here to me," he said.

Verse 19—Then he directed the people to sit down on the grass. Taking the five loaves and the two fish and looking up to heaven, he gave thanks and broke the loaves. Then he gave them to the disciples, and the disciples gave them to the people.

Verse 20—They ate and were satisfied, and the disciples picked up twelve basketfuls of broken pieces that were left over.

Verse 21—The number of those who ate was about five thousand men, besides women and children.

Matthew 15:29-38

Verse 29—Jesus left there and went along the Sea of Galilee. Then he went up on a mountainside and sat down.

Verse 30—Great crowds came to him, bringing the lame, the blind, the crippled, the mute and many others, and laid them at his feet; and he healed them.

Verse 31—The people were amazed when they saw the mute speaking, the crippled made well, the lame walking and the blind seeing. And they praised the God of Israel.

Verse 32—Jesus called his disciples to him and said, "I have compassion for these people; they have already been with me three days and have nothing to eat. I do not want to send them away hungry, or they may collapse on the way."

Verse 33—His disciples answered, "Where could we get enough bread in this remote place to feed such a crowd?"

Verse 34—"How many loaves do you have?" Jesus asked.
"Seven," they replied, "and a few small fish."

Verse 35—He told the crowd to sit down on the ground.

Verse 36—Then he took the seven loaves and the fish, and when he had given thanks, he broke them and gave them to the disciples and they in turn to the people.

Verse 37—They all ate and were satisfied. Afterward the disciples picked up seven basketfuls of broken pieces that were left over.

Verse 38—The number of those who ate was four thousand, besides women and children.

- Search the passages, and circle every phrase that indicates Jesus cares about people.
- Underline every phrase that indicates what made Jesus able to provide food for the people.
- Put a star beside the sentence in each passage that means the most to you.
- Below, write two or three sentences explaining what Jesus' miracle of meeting needs means for us today.

Sheep and Shepherd

Purpose:

Students will learn why Jesus wants them to be his followers.

Supplies:

You'll need Bibles, blindfolds, poster board, markers, and tape.

Experience:

Ask for a volunteer, but don't explain what he or she will do. Gather the rest of the class on one side of the room. Create an obstacle course between the group and a designated area on the opposite side, using furniture and other materials in the room.

Tell the class: **You're going to walk from one side of the room to the other, but you're going to be blindfolded, so it'll be a little tougher than usual. To make things easier for you, keep saying "baa" like a sheep. This way, you'll find out where other people are. Our volunteer will serve as your "shepherd." This person will help you by gently bumping you in the right direction and calling out directions. The shepherd can't use his or her hands, however, or tell you anything except directions such as "over here" or "turn right." This activity will end when all of you are safely herded over to the "corral."**

Point out a place at the other end of the room to be the corral. Blindfold everyone but the shepherd, making sure blindfolded students can't see. Then start the activity.

While this is going on, make things tougher for the students by nudging them the wrong way, getting in their way, and changing the course. If you have more than twelve people, you might want to try using two or more shepherds and corrals, and having the sheep identify themselves as belonging to their respective flocks by "baaing" differently.

After all the sheep have made it to the corral, ask:

● **What was it like to be a sheep?** *(I felt helpless; confusing; aggravating; fun.)*

● **What was it like to be a shepherd?** *(I had power; I was needed; I was busy.)*

● **How did the sheep feel about the shepherd?** *(Dependent; grateful; ungrateful.)*

● **How did you react when you realized someone was turning you the wrong way?** *(I was angry; I got confused.)*

● **How is being a Christian like being a sheep?** *(We're dependent on Jesus; Christians will wander without God's direction.)*

● **What does this activity teach us about our relationship with Jesus?** *(We're dependent on him; we can wander off if we want to; Jesus is gentle; there are obstacles; other people or things interfere.)*

● **What specific things can we do to be better "sheep"?** *(Listen to God more; follow God's directions; stay close to the rest of Jesus' flock.)*

● **How is being turned the wrong way in the activity like being led away from our faith as Christians?** *(People try to get us to do wrong things; sometimes we don't watch where we're going and end up doing something wrong.)*

Tape a large sheet of poster board to the wall. Give students each a marker and a Bible. Say: **John was very concerned with the "flock" of believers he was a member of, and this concern showed up in everything he wrote. We can better understand what it means to belong to Jesus' flock by looking at what John had to say.**

Form five groups of one or more, and assign each group a chapter in 1 John. Have groups each look in their chapter for qualities or behaviors that describe a Christian sheep. Have groups write or draw something on the poster board to express their discoveries. They can write a single word; compose a poem; draw a picture; or do anything else they think will get the point across.

While they're looking things up, write "How to Spot a Sheep" on the poster board in big letters. Allow groups up to ten minutes to read their chapters, discuss them, and write or draw on the poster board. Then have groups each explain what they wrote or drew after everyone is done.

Have someone read aloud John 10:1-18.

● **According to Jesus' message in this passage, what does it mean to be Jesus' sheep?** *(We're to love him and do his will; Jesus loves us and will lead us.)*

● **Is it always easy being a sheep? Explain.** *(Yes, I'm totally committed to God; no, sometimes I'm tempted to do wrong things.)*

Say: **Being a sheep isn't always easy. But Jesus wants us to be his sheep. Thankfully, even when we fail, Jesus loves us just the same.**

Spending Money

Purpose:

Students will explore what it means to have a giving heart.

Supplies:

You'll need Bibles, paper, pencils, newsprint, markers, tape, and one hundred dollars in play money from the "Money" handout (p. 97) for each of three groups.

Experience:

Form three groups. Give each group one hundred dollars in play money. Tell students that each group must decide how to spend its money. Tell students to use the money to help needy people in some way.

When groups are ready, have them share their plans. Then ask:

● **How difficult was your task?** *(It was hard to agree on what to do with it; it wasn't enough money to really make a difference.)*

● **How would your decision change if you had real money instead of play money?** *(It wouldn't change at all; I'd probably spend the money on clothes.)*

● **Is it harder to give real money rather than play money? Why?** *(Because the paper money doesn't really cost you anything; because I need the real money for myself.)*

● **How is the play money like our attitude toward giving?** *(It looks good, but it doesn't have any real substance; we sometimes make promises to give and then don't keep them.)*

Say: **Let's try something a little more challenging. It costs about twenty-four dollars to feed and clothe a child for one month. We could probably feed and clothe a child with money you have with you now. I'm going to pass around a hat. I want to challenge you to give up money so we can change a life halfway around the world.**

Pass around the hat, and count the money that you collect. Be sensitive to students who may not carry money or may not have money they can give away. Encourage group members to give only if they are able and not to feel bad if they don't.

If your group does not collect the twenty-four dollars, consider making up the difference yourself or asking the church to do it.

Compassion International will accept your one-time gift to feed and clothe one of the children they support. Arrange for your group to mail the money to: Compassion International, P.O. Box 7000, Colorado Springs, CO 80933.

Ask:

● **How do you feel now that you have sacrificed real money?** *(I feel good; I wonder how I'm going to pay for lunch tomorrow.)*

● **How is the way you feel now different from the way you felt when you spent the play money?** *(I know what I'm doing is making a difference now; I feel like I've really given up something.)*

● **How is the second activity like really living for Christ?** *(It involved sacrifice; we helped someone else.)*

Say: **God wants each of us to develop a giving heart. Let's take a closer look at just what that means.**

According to 2 Corinthians, Paul was involved in taking up an offering for people who were starving. Some were giving more than they were really able to give. Others were not really giving at all. Let's look at what Paul wrote to the Christians in Corinth.

Form two groups—Macedonians and Corinthians. Ask the groups to read 2 Corinthians 8:1-15. Instruct them each to prepare a presentation that defends their assigned church's actions concerning giving. Have groups give their presentations. Encourage groups to include all their members in the presentations.

After the presentations, ask:

● **Which position comes closest to the way you feel about giving?**

● **Which position is the one God encourages?**

● **Why does God want us to be generous givers?** *(Because God is a generous giver; because it's the right thing to do.)*

Distribute pencils and paper. Instruct students to read 2 Corinthians 9:6-15 silently. Ask students each to write one sentence that summarizes what Paul is saying. Have volunteers tell what they wrote. Have students vote on which sentence best summarizes Paul's message. Write that sentence on a sheet of newsprint with a marker and tape it to the wall.

Say: **God wants us to have giving hearts because he knows that giving to others will in turn bless us.**

Money

Sundae Suffering

Purpose:

Teenagers will discover more about the depth of Jesus' love for us by understanding what he went through on the cross.

Supplies:

You'll need Bibles, pencils, a folding chair, a sheet of plastic, ice cream, toppings, towels, a ⅜ x 10-inch nail, a hammer, and one copy of the "Crucifixion Quiz" handout (p. 101) for each person.

Experience:

Form two teams, and name one person to represent each team in a Bible quiz.

Say: **The job of each team is to cheer its representative on to victory. You may coach your representative if you think you know the right answer, but only the representative may tell me the answer.**

Do *not* explain the punishment before a team selects a representative, and don't let anyone switch places with a representative at this point.

Say: **Because the whole team is counting on him** (or her)**, the losing representative will be "punished" by being turned into a human ice cream sundae.**

Play the game by asking the following questions about Easter. The first person to answer correctly gets one point, and the first person with three points wins. If students seem to be having trouble answering the questions, team members may look for answers in their Bibles during the quiz.

Ask:

● **What did the soldiers use to make a crown for Jesus?** *(Thorny branches.)*

● **What's one of the ways the soldiers tortured Jesus before killing him?** *(Beating him with sticks; whipping him; spitting on him.)*

● **What was the name of the governor who allowed Jesus to be killed?** *(Pilate.)*

● **How many robbers were crucified alongside Jesus?** *(Two.)*

● **What was the name of the man who buried Jesus?** *(Joseph of Arimathea.)*

● **Who was the first person to see Jesus after he rose from the**

dead? *(Mary Magdalene.)*

After you have declared a winner, have the losing representative prepare for "punishment." Have him or her sit on a folding chair with a sheet of plastic underneath to protect the floor. Bring out ice cream and toppings such as chocolate syrup, whipped cream, and, of course, a cherry. Laugh and joke about what a mess you're going to make of this person's hair and clothes.

Just before making the "sundae," have another leader or student who's agreed ahead of time come forward and volunteer to take the punishment for the losing representative. Have them trade places, then proceed to make the ice cream sundae on the volunteer's head. The volunteer will obviously be uncomfortable, but it will not hurt him or her.

When you're finished, have everyone cheer for the volunteer, then send him or her out to clean up. (Have plenty of towels handy.)

Ask the losing representative:

● **How did it make you feel to let someone else suffer in your place?** *(I was relieved; I felt guilty; thankful.)*

Ask the class:

● **What were you thinking as you watched an innocent person suffer?** *(I felt sorry; I'm glad it wasn't me; I didn't think it was fair.)*

● **How was this activity like what Jesus did on the cross?** *(He chose to take our punishment for us; he suffered so we wouldn't have to.)*

● **Why did Jesus have to die?** *(So we wouldn't have to suffer; so we could have a relationship with God; so we could go to heaven.)*

● **How does it make you feel to know that Jesus took your place on the cross?** *(Relieved; guilty; thankful.)*

● **How do you think the people closest to Jesus must have felt as they watched him suffer and die?** *(Sorry; confused; they didn't think it was fair; sad.)*

Read John 3:16.

Say: **We can see from this exercise how fortunate we are that Christ took our punishment for us. But we can't truly appreciate the depth of his love until we can better understand just how much he suffered for us.**

Have students open their Bibles to Mark 15:16-37.

Say: **As I read this passage aloud, follow along in your Bibles. Each time I come to a place where a group of people, such as soldiers, are speaking, I'll stop. At that point everyone should read aloud what the people were saying. Say the words with feeling, as if you were really there.**

(Don't worry if students read from various versions of the Bible. This will give the reading more of a "crowd" effect with everyone calling out at once.)

Read the passage aloud, stopping during verses 18, 29-30, 31-32, and 35-36

Answers to "Crucifixion Quiz"

1. FALSE. Jesus was whipped with a cat-o'-nine-tails. This whip had nine straps, and each strap usually had a piece of glass, metal, or a sharp stone at the tip which was dragged across the victim's back with each lash.

2. FALSE. Crosses were close enough to the ground to allow spectators to hit the victims, poke them with sticks, or spit on them.

3. TRUE. The nails probably went between the two bones in his wrists and into the feet right above the heels.

4. FALSE. Most likely, he suffocated. As the cross was lifted vertically and dropped into its stand, it was common for the victim's arms to pop out of their sockets. The rib cage then pressed against the lungs, making breathing almost impossible. Victims would have to pull themselves up on their dislocated arms and pierced hands just to take a breath or speak, then they would collapse once again.

5. TRUE. This was to further humiliate the victim. Soldiers gambled for Jesus' clothes at the foot of the cross.

6. FALSE. The Bible makes it clear that although Jesus was God, he was also fully human. He got hungry, thirsty, and tired. He felt the pain of the cross the same way you or I would.

7. TRUE. He had to endure the cruelty and mocking of the very people he was dying for. His closest friends had abandoned him. And worst of all, for that brief moment in history when he took our sins upon himself, even God turned away.

for students to speak. As you read, pass a ⅜ x 10-inch nail around the room to give students an idea of what went into Christ's hands and feet. (These nails can be purchased in hardware stores for about fifty cents apiece.) Also, have another leader in the back of the room pound a hammer every three or four seconds.

After reading the Scripture, give each student a pencil and a photocopy of the "Crucifixion Quiz" handout (p. 101). Have students form groups of no more than four and work together on the quiz. After several minutes regroup to go over the answers. Before explaining the correct responses, have groups explain their answers. Use the key in the margin to fill in information students may be unaware of.

Ask:

● **How has this reading and quiz made you feel about Jesus' death?** *(Sad; sick because of the way he was treated; disgusted.)*

● **Why do you think Jesus was willing to endure this?** *(Because he loved us; because he knew what the outcome would be; he knew he'd come back to life.)*

● **If you had to die in the same fashion as Jesus, is there anyone or anything you would still die for? Why or why not?** *(Yes, I love someone that much; no, I don't think I could go through that for anyone.)*

● **How does knowing what Jesus went through for you make you feel about him?** *(It makes me have more respect for him; it makes me more thankful; I feel really loved by God.)*

Say: **Knowing what Christ went through can help us understand the depth of his love for us. Any innocent person who would go through this torture must have incredible love for others.**

Crucifixion Quiz

Discuss these statements in your groups and answer either true or false to each one.

_____ 1. When Jesus was whipped thirty-nine lashes, the whip used was much like the bullwhips we see today.

_____ 2. The cross hung high over everyone's head.

_____ 3. Nails were driven through Jesus' hands or wrists and feet, and when the cross was lifted, all his weight rested on these nail-pierced wounds.

_____ 4. Jesus probably bled to death.

_____ 5. Jesus was probably naked, or at least nearly naked, as he hung on the cross.

_____ 6. Since Jesus was the Son of God, he didn't feel pain the same way we would.

_____ 7. The greatest pain Jesus suffered on the cross probably wasn't physical pain, but emotional pain.

To Win or Be Faithful

Purpose:

Students will learn from Joseph's story why faithfulness is important to God.

Supplies:

You'll need Bibles, index cards, and pencils.

Experience:

Form groups of six or fewer. Give students each two index cards and a pencil. Tell kids to put an X on one card and an O on the other and then to hold the cards where no one else can see the markings.

Say: **We're going to play a little game. The person with the most points at the end wins. Here's how it works. In each round of the game, we're going to have each of you reveal either your X or your O. Before you reveal any cards, you can talk together in your group to decide which letter your group will reveal. Then you'll each select the card you really want to reveal, hold it out face down, and turn it over when I say to.**

Now here's the way the game is scored. If every person in your group reveals the same card, each of your group's members will get one hundred points. If only one person reveals the opposite letter, he or she gets five hundred points and the others each get one hundred. But if more than one person reveals the opposite letter, those people each get only twenty-five points, while the rest of the group gets one hundred points each.

Remember, the person with the most points wins.

Give each group a third index card so they can keep score. Tell groups to keep score carefully and announce the score after each round. Be sure to participate in a group yourself. Play several rounds of the game.

If no one breaks from the group's decision after two or three rounds, do it yourself. Play at least a round or two after the first person breaks from the group.

After several rounds, stop the game. Ask:

● **What went through your mind when you were deciding which card to show?** *(I thought about winning the most points; I didn't know what I wanted to do.)*

● **How hard was it to stick with the group when you knew you might get five hundred points by going against them?** *(Tough, I wanted to win; not bad, I wanted to play it safe.)*

● **How is the way you felt in choosing whether to be faithful to the group like Joseph might have felt in choosing to be faithful to God?** *(Sometimes it's easy to be tempted; sometimes we get selfish.)*

Say: **In this game it may have been tough for us to be faithful to our groups because of what we could win for ourselves. Joseph was faithful to God in much tougher situations than this game. But he stayed faithful, even when it was hard to see that God was helping him.**

Form two groups. Designate one group to be Joseph's lawyers and the other group to be his spiritual advisors.

Say: **I'm going to read some situations from Joseph's life in the Bible. Listen carefully because after I read each section, you'll be given a chance to advise Joseph. The lawyers group should keep Joseph's success in mind at all times. The spiritual advisors group should keep Joseph's relationship with God in mind at all times.**

Read each passage listed here, pausing after each one to give each group thirty seconds to advise Joseph about what he should do:

● Genesis 37:12-28
● Genesis 39:1-20a
● Genesis 40:1-23
● Genesis 41:39-41; 41:56–42:6

After students have advised Joseph on all of the situations, ask:

● **What did Joseph do in each of these situations?** *(Check out Genesis 39:2-4, 21-23; 41:15-16; and 45:1-11 if students don't know how Joseph actually responded.)*

● **Whose advice did he follow more closely, his lawyers or his spiritual advisors? Explain.** *(His spiritual advisors, since he did what God wanted; he always did what he knew was right.)*

● **How easy do you think it was for Joseph to be faithful to God in each of those situations? Explain.** *(Easy, his faith was strong; tough, he faced strong temptations.)*

Say: **Joseph was a true hero because he stayed faithful to God no matter what happened—and some pretty bad things happened to him. His example can help us know that staying faithful to God is not only possible, it's the best way to grow closer to God.**

Tough Questions

Purpose:

Students will explore how a variety of resources can help them study the Bible.

Supplies:

You'll need Bibles, pencils, paper, one photocopy of the "Tough Trivia" handout (p. 107) for each group of three or four, and one photocopy of the "What Do I Do With This?" handout (p. 108) for each person. You'll also need reference tools such as a dictionary and a copy of yesterday's newspaper, and biblical reference tools such as a concordance, a study Bible, a Bible commentary, a Bible dictionary, and a Bible encyclopedia.

Experience:

Form groups of three or four. Give each group a "Tough Trivia" handout (p. 107) and pencils. Tell students they have three minutes to find all the answers. Allow them to use a dictionary, yesterday's newspaper, and any other reference tools you brought.

After three minutes, call time and give the answers from the "Answers to Tough Trivia" box below. Have groups each report how many questions they answered correctly.

Then ask:

Answers to Tough Trivia

1. (Check yesterday's newspaper.)
2. 1799
3. Walter Mondale
4. 5,280
5. (Check local TV listings.)
6. a fictitious name
7. Asia
8. Tennessee Valley Authority
9. abacus
10. one-twelfth

● **How tough was it to find the answers?** *(Easy, we just didn't have time; hard, we didn't know where to look.)*

● **What tools did you use to help you find the answers?** *(The dictionary; the newspaper.)*

● **How is finding those answers like finding answers in the Bible?** *(Sometimes you just don't know where to look; answers you're looking for just aren't there.)*

● **What tools might one use to help find answers in the Bible?** *(A concordance; a Bible dictionary.)*

Say: **There are several tools that can help**

us find what we're looking for in the Bible. Let's look at a few of the most helpful ones.

Pass around a Bible concordance (one found in the back of a Bible would work fine), a study Bible or a Bible commentary, and a Bible dictionary or encyclopedia. Check with your pastor to find these books. Or contact a local library to see if they have any available. If you have more than ten kids, consider bringing more than one example of each.

Give students Bibles and the "What Do I Do With This?" handouts (p. 108). Briefly review the handout with your class.

Say: **To get us started using these Bible study tools, I'm going to let you find the passages we'll study today. I'll give you hints, and let you use the tools we have here to find the Scriptures.**

Give the following hints as needed until students find the verses on their own. The hints are based on the New International Version of the Bible. If you use a different version, adjust your hints to fit your version. If students have trouble deciding which tool to use, suggest they start with a concordance. But don't give them the references.

● **2 Timothy 2:15 hints:**
(a) contains the word "workman"
(b) contains the word "truth"
(c) is in the New Testament
(d) is in one of the books Paul wrote
(e) is in 2 Timothy
(f) starts out, "Do your best to present yourself to God as one approved."

● **2 Peter 3:15-18 hints:**
(a) contains the word "Scriptures"
(b) contains the word "Paul"
(c) is in the New Testament
(d) is in one of the books Peter wrote
(e) is in 2 Peter
(f) starts out, "Bear in mind that our Lord's patience means salvation."

When students have tracked down the verses, form two groups. If you have more than ten students, form enough groups so you have no more than five students in each group. Have each group study one of the two passages.

Say: **In your group, read your passage and discuss what it means. Then use the tools we have here to find out more about your passage. Record your findings on paper.**

Be sure each group has access to the Bible study tools mentioned on the "What Do I Do With This?" handout. Give each group paper and pencils. Then let them search for about ten minutes. Circulate around the room, giving suggestions to groups having trouble.

After ten minutes, have groups report what they found.

Then ask:

● **What's the main message of 2 Timothy 2:15?** *(It's important to understand what's in the Bible; God will be pleased if we study his Word well.)*

● **What's the main message of 2 Peter 3:15-18?** *(The words of Scripture are from God; some things are hard to understand.)*

● **How did the tools you used help you understand the Scriptures better?** *(They gave us new information; they helped us understand phrases that weren't clear to us.)*

Say: **With these tools and the guidance of the Holy Spirit, we can study and learn what the Bible teaches about all aspects of life.**

Tough Trivia

1. What was the official high temperature the day before yesterday?

2. What year did George Washington die?

3. Who was vice president under Jimmy Carter?

4. How many feet are in a mile?

5. What TV show was on NBC at 9:00 last night?

6. What's a pseudonym?

7. Of the seven continents, which is largest in area?

8. What does TVA stand for?

9. What's a Chinese counting device made up of beads that slide on wires?

10. What proportion of a pound is a troy ounce?

What Do I Do With This?

The following tools can help you study the Bible. Read through this sheet to see how each tool can help you, then keep this sheet handy at home for future reference.

Bible Concordance

What it does.

A concordance lists words from the Bible in alphabetical order, and then tells where those words appear in the Bible. Some big, unabridged concordances contain every word in every verse of the Bible. Others, such as those in the back of many Bibles, contain only the most significant words in verses.

How you can use it.

You can use a concordance for at least two purposes. One is to find places in the Bible where a particular word is used. For example, if you want to read verses that mention "sin," look up "sin" in your concordance, then look up the Bible references listed there.

Concordances can also help you find passages you "kind of" know but aren't sure where they are. For example, if you remember a verse that says something about God loving the world but don't know where to find it, you can look up "love" in your concordance. If you remember other words from the verse, you can look them up too. Before long you'll track down your verse: John 3:16.

Bible Dictionary or Bible Encyclopedia

What it does.

A Bible dictionary or encyclopedia lists biblical topics, people, and places in alphabetical order. For each item listed, it gives historical information and explains the topics to help you understand the Bible better.

How you can use it.

You can use a Bible dictionary to help you learn about people, places, or things in the Bible. For example, suppose you want to find out who the Apostle Paul was. You can look up "Paul" in a Bible dictionary, and it'll provide information about who Paul was and what he did.

A Study Bible or Bible Commentary

What it does.

A study Bible or Bible commentary follows Scripture and gives comments to help us understand passages and words in the Bible. A study Bible usually covers the whole Bible. A commentary may cover the whole Bible, the Old or New Testament, or only one book of the Bible.

How you can use it.

You can use study Bibles or Bible commentaries to help you understand parts of Scripture. For example, if you're not sure what Jesus means in John 4:10 when he talks about "living water," you could look up that verse in a study Bible or commentary to help you understand it.

Tough Times

Purpose:

Teenagers will discover how tough times can make them stronger.

Supplies:

You'll need Bibles, pencils, newsprint, tape, markers, and one "Paul and the Philippian Adventure!" handout (p. 112) for each person.

Experience:

Before your meeting, write each one of the following situations on a separate sheet of newsprint.

- You've just backed your folks' car into a tree.
- Your best friend has just been caught cheating on a test.
- Your boyfriend or girlfriend is breaking up with you.
- Your math teacher is being unfair to you for no reason.
- You've just found out your favorite uncle has a drug problem.
- Your baby brother has just puked on your outfit minutes before you're supposed to leave for the big dance.
- Your youth pastor has just resigned.
- Your civics class is going on a really great field trip, but you can't go because you have to get your braces adjusted.
- You've recently lost your job and now have no money for a social life.
- Your parents have just told you that you'll all be moving so your dad can take a new job.

Tape the signs on the wall in various places around the room with blank sheets of newsprint beside them.

After students arrive, form groups of three or fewer. Provide a marker for each group, and say: **You are now going to be faced with an obstacle course of tough situations. Each group will start at a different sign. At each station you must come up with something good that could come from that situation. Write it on the newsprint. You may not use what another group has already written. If you finish every station, take your group and sit down in the middle of the room. You have five minutes. Go!**

Keep the students moving. After five minutes, call the students together.

Ask:

● **What went through your mind while you were dealing with the problems in the room?** *(I was frustrated; I was glad to come up with something good; I felt pressured; I was relieved.)*

● **Which situation was the hardest to resolve? What made it hard?**

● **Which situation ended up being the most fun? Explain.**

● **What effect does attitude have when facing a difficult situation?** *(It might make it easier to face; one might be able to grow more from the situation; one might develop an unrealistic approach to life.)*

● **How do you normally respond to tough times?** *(I cry; I get depressed; I get mad; I try to get through it as fast as possible.)*

● **How do you think God would like us to respond?** *(Trust him to get us through it; keep a positive attitude; overcome our troubles.)*

Say: **We are not the only ones who have had to face difficult situations. Let's look at the Scriptures to find out about someone else who went through a trial.**

Read aloud Acts 16:16-34. (Be sure to read it dramatically, not in a monotone.) Then give a "Paul and the Philippian Adventure!" handout (p. 112), a Bible, and a pencil to each student.

Say: **Paul had his share of tough times. Some of his life sounds like an adventure movie. Before a movie is shot, the people creating it draw up what is called a "storyboard." A storyboard is a series of rough sketches to show what they want in each shot. Today we're going to draw up a storyboard for this story out of Paul's life. Use the handout to make your own storyboard. You may work alone or in pairs. Stick figures are acceptable. Now let's make a storyboard.**

Allow the students a few minutes to draw up their storyboards. Encourage them not to be fancy with their art, just to get down on paper what they would want a scene to show. If they want to include more scenes, have them draw on the back of the handout.

When everyone is finished, allow volunteers to share their storyboards with the group.

Then ask:

● **How would you have felt if you had been in Paul's place in this situation?** *(Angry; scared; hopeless; depressed.)*

● **Which of the situations from Paul's life would have been hardest to have a positive attitude about? Explain.** *(Being put in jail; being publicly beaten; being falsely accused.)*

● **Why do you think Paul was able to find joy in the middle of his sufferings?** *(His attitude was really good; he was used to God helping him out; he'd learned to roll with the punches while he trusted God.)*

● **How can our lives and attitudes be like Paul's?** *(We can trust God* *to take care of us; we can try not to let our circumstances affect our attitude.)*

Say: **Paul consistently found joy in tough situations. Peter gives us an idea of the result of a lifestyle like that. Read silently 1 Peter 1:6-9.**

Allow the class time to read the passage. Then have as many volunteers as possible sum up the passage in their own words.

After several have shared, ask:

● **What reasons did Peter give for finding joy in tough situations?** *(We're receiving the goal of our faith; we're growing; our faith may be proved genuine; God will be glorified by us; we'll receive our salvation.)*

● **What is hard about rejoicing in tough times?** *(We're hurting; we don't feel like rejoicing; we think God may have let us down.)*

Say: **The Bible teaches that tough times can make us stronger and because of that we can rejoice.**

Paul and the Philippian Adventure!

Read Acts 16:16-34, and prepare a storyboard for a film based on this passage.
Include rough sketches (stick figures are OK) and an outline of
what things you would include in each scene.

OPENING SCENE	SCENE 4
Scene summary: _____	Scene summary: _____

SCENE 2	SCENE 5
Scene summary: _____	Scene summary: _____

SCENE 3	CLOSING SCENE
Scene summary: _____	Scene summary: _____

Trust Me

Purpose:

Teenagers will explore what the Bible says about demons.

Supplies:

You'll need Bibles and five strips each of blue, red, and green paper.

Experience:

Ask for three volunteers. Give one volunteer five strips of blue paper, another five strips of red paper, and the last one five strips of green paper. Send them out of the room.

Form three teams with the remaining students, and label them blue, red, and green. Have team members intermingle and then form a circle around the room.

Say: **Each volunteer has five strips of colored paper to distribute to his or her respective team members. The problem is they don't know who their team members are. You must try to convince each of the three that you're on his or her team and get a strip of paper from him or her. The team getting the most strips of paper wins.**

Bring in the volunteers.

Say to them: **Distribute your strips of paper to those who you think are your team members.**

When the strips have been passed out, have students re-form their teams and count their strips. The team with the most wins.

Ask:

● **Volunteers, what was it like trying to decide who to listen to? Explain.** *(I felt nervous, I didn't want to make the wrong choice; confused, they all were saying they were on my team.)*

● **Team members, what was it like trying to convince the volunteers you were on their team? Explain.** *(Frustrating, I couldn't convince our team's volunteer that I was telling the truth; I felt guilty trying to get someone to believe my lie.)*

● **How is life like this game?** *(We don't always know who to believe; we get a lot of mixed messages.)*

● **Many people believe unseen demons around us try to influence us in wrong ways. What do you think about demons?** *(I don't think they're real; I think they're scary in movies; I think demons are real.)*

● **If demons *were* to influence us, how would their actions be like this game?** *(They'd try to control our thoughts; they'd surround us with confusing messages.)*

Say: **The idea of unseen beings around us trying to get us to sin can be scary. Let's see what the Bible says about demons.**

Form three groups, and give each group at least one Bible. Assign each group Scriptures as follows:

Group 1: Matthew 24:4; 1 Timothy 4:1-2; and James 4:7.

Group 2: Acts 13:8-10; Ephesians 4:27; and Revelation 12:7-9.

Group 3: John 8:42-45; 2 Corinthians 11:14-15; and Ephesians 6:10-18.

Say: **Read your Scriptures; and determine what the Bible says demons are, what they do, and how to fight against them.**

Allow about five minutes for groups to read and discuss their passages.

Say: **Stand while I ask a question. When someone answers, sit down if you agree and have nothing to add. If you disagree or have more information, tell us. Then those who have nothing to add may also sit down. We'll continue until everyone is sitting; then I'll ask a new question.**

Be sure everyone is standing before each new question.

Ask:

● **From what you've read, what do you think demons are?** *(Angels following Satan; evil spirits.)*

● **Some of your passages were about Satan, or the devil, and some were about demons. What's the difference?** *(Demons follow the devil's orders; Satan uses demons to do his work; demons are like little devils.)*

● **What does the Bible say demons' goals are?** *(To lie to us; to keep us from God; to turn people away from their faith; to trick people.)*

● **How could they do this?** *(Make us question whether God's real; make us think we're not worth anything; fill our minds with wrong thoughts.)*

● **Do you think demons are around and influencing us today? Explain.** *(Yes, the Bible talks about their role in future events; yes, it would explain all the evil in the world; no, people just use them as an excuse to do wrong.)*

● **Do you think every time we sin it's because of demons? Explain.** *(Yes, they cause evil; no, they just try to keep us from God; no, we still have a choice in our actions.)*

● **What ways does the Bible suggest we fight against evil?** *(Use God's armor; run away from evil; resist the devil.)*

● **After reading these Scriptures, has your opinion of demons** changed? **Why or why not?** *(Yes, they're more dangerous than I thought; yes, I think they're real now; no, I still think they're a thing of the past.)*

Say: **Whether you believe in demons or not, evil is a real problem. Thankfully, God can give us the wisdom to avoid evil and the strength to overcome it.**

The Vine

Purpose:

Teenagers will learn why it's important to produce fruit as Christians.

Supplies:

You'll need Bibles, pencils, paper towels, one empty cup for each person, one clean and sanitary bucket of water, one clean and sanitary empty bucket, a thin rope, tape, and one copy of the "Fruit of the Vine" handout (p. 118) for each group of four or five.

Experience:

Place the bucket with the water in it on the opposite side of the room from the empty bucket. Have the group members line up between the two buckets with you in the middle and everyone holding a cup.

Tell the class: **We're going to take the water out of this bucket and put it into the bucket at the other end of the line. The object is to move as much water as possible from the full bucket into the empty bucket. To do this, the person closest to the water bucket will take a cup, dip it into the bucket, and then pour it into the cup of the person next to them. This person will pour it into the next person's cup, and so on, until the last person pours it into the bucket at the end.**

Keep the water flowing as smoothly as possible. When the empty bucket is about half full, start taking large sips out of your cup as the water goes by. When the first bucket is out of water, stop the activity. Have paper towels available for cleanup.

Ask:

● **What went well in this exercise?** *(We completed the task; we didn't spill much.)*

● **What hindered our progress?** *(You kept drinking the water; people kept spilling the water.)*

● **What thoughts did you have when someone drank or spilled the water? Explain.** *(I was angry, he or she wasn't careful; I felt frustrated, I was doing my job so why couldn't everyone?)*

● **If you were to look at the first bucket as Jesus and the other bucket as non-Christians, what might the water represent?** *(God's love;*

Jesus' teachings; the Bible.)

● **What does this activity say about the role of Christians?** *(We're responsible to get Jesus' love to people; some of us detract from the process by taking Jesus' love in but not producing anything.)*

Say: **When we become Christians, we accept not only Jesus' love but also Jesus' command for us to share that love with others.**

Have someone read aloud Isaiah 5:1-7 and John 15:1-17.

Ask:

● **What do these passages suggest about our relationship with Jesus and our relationships with others?** *(We're to lean on Jesus for strength; Jesus wants us to share his love with others; we have a responsibility to be Jesus' branches.)*

● **What does Jesus mean when he says he's the vine and we're the branches?** *(Jesus is the source of all life and love; Jesus is the center of our lives.)*

● **What can we learn from Jesus' teaching in John 15:1-17 to help us be better followers?** *(Rely on Jesus; show love to others.)*

● **What does it mean to "bear fruit"?** *(To share Jesus with others; to do good things for people; to love other people.)*

Tape a thin rope to the ceiling or high on a wall. Form groups of no more than five. Distribute copies of the "Fruit of the Vine" handout (p. 118) and pencils to each group.

Say: **Being Jesus' branches requires certain things of us. Many of these are described in the book of James. In your groups, read aloud James 3–4 and determine actions, attitudes, and attributes associated with being Jesus' branches. List each item in the branch on one of the handouts.**

Allow groups up to five minutes to read James 3–4 and write in the handouts. Then give groups tape to attach their handouts to the rope. Have kids walk around the "vine" and silently read the words written on the branches.

Say: **Without the branches we added, this vine couldn't produce fruit. Yet producing fruit is an important responsibility we have as Christians.**

Fruit of the Vine

What's Your Problem?

Purpose:

Teenagers will study the Christmas story to see how God has everything under control, even if we don't.

Supplies:

You'll need Bibles, a photocopy of the "Problems" slips (p. 122), an orange, tape, newsprint, a marker, paper, and pencils.

Experience:

Before class, photocopy and cut apart the "Problems" slips (p. 122). You'll need to give one slip to each group in this activity.

Form three groups. Ask for a volunteer from each group. Tell the volunteers you'll be giving them each secret instructions.

To the volunteer from the first group, give the Problem 1 slip and the orange. To the volunteer from the second group, give the Problem 2 slip. To the third volunteer, give the Problem 3 slip.

Tell the first and third groups to begin; then ask the second volunteer to decide whether he or she wants help with the math problems. If the student says yes, allow a few seconds for the group to receive sheets of paper and pencils and to copy their respective math problems from the slip. Then give the start signal and allow thirty seconds for group members to solve their problems. After thirty seconds, check their answers against the following key:

1. 768,060
2. 7,056
3. 5.13
4. 13.33
5. 94.125
6. 535,500

Encourage the other groups to finish quickly. When you call the activity to a close, have groups stay together. Ask the volunteers who are holding the problem slips to read them aloud.

Ask the volunteers:

● **What were your feelings during the exercise?** *(I felt put on the spot; I was worried I wouldn't do the right thing; embarrassment.)*

● **How is that like the way you feel when you're in the middle of a difficult situation?** *(It's the same, I feel uncomfortable; it's similar, I wonder if I'll do things right.)*

Ask the rest of the class:

● **How did the rest of you feel?** *(Curious about what was on the slips; wondering what I'd be asked to do.)*

● **What decisions had to be made about your group's problem by the person holding the slip?** *(How much help to get from the group; whether to trust the group's answers.)*

● **What was easier about working on the problems as a group?** *(The work could be split up among the group; some decisions could be talked over.)*

● **What was harder about working as a group?** *(We didn't always agree about how to solve the problem; I could've solved the problem more quickly by myself.)*

● **What did this exercise reveal about problems we face?** *(Sometimes they're forced on us; decisions have to be made to deal with them successfully.)*

Congratulate the groups for their efforts, and say: **Sometimes you have to make tough decisions about problems. Let's take a look at some characters from the Christmas story, and check out the decisions they had to make about the problems facing them.**

Assign volunteers one of the following Bible passages to read aloud: Isaiah 7:14 and Micah 5:2. Ask:

● **Have you ever heard these verses before? If so, what context did you hear them in?** *(At church during the Christmas season; in a sermon.)*

Say: **These verses help us see that God knew what he was going to do long before it ever happened.**

Then ask:

● **How could it help you to know God has a plan for everything that happens long before it comes to pass?** *(It could help me to not panic; it could help me pray more often about my future.)*

Have the remaining volunteers read aloud Luke 1:5-80.

Tape a sheet of newsprint on the wall. Using a marker, create on the newsprint a grid similar to the illustration below.

Character	Problem	How Resolved	What Helped

Ask for a volunteer to be secretary for the class. To involve more students, choose a different secretary for each character you discuss. Go through the Luke passage, and list on the newsprint the different characters as they appear in the Scripture. For each character, have students respond to each of these questions:

- **What problem(s) did this person face?**
- **Were the problem(s) resolved? If so, how?**
- **What helped to resolve the problem?**

Say: **Just like the people from the Christmas story, our lives today aren't in nice, neat packages. But God knew a long time ago how all the confusing details would work together to fit his plan. If we can keep trusting God through all the confusion, we'll see God still has everything under control, even if we don't.**

Problems

Problem 1

Your problem involves the orange. What do you do with it? Divide it and share it with everyone else? Eat it yourself? Or give it to someone else and let that person worry about it?

Problem 2

In a few minutes, I'll give you a signal after which you'll have thirty seconds to complete the following six math problems. That's five seconds per problem. You're on your honor not to work on the problems until I give you the signal. Before I signal you, you have to decide whether you want help from the rest of your group to get the problems done on time. Think about it!

1. $8,534 \times 90 = ?$
2. $24 \times 147 \times 2 = ?$
3. $118 \div 23 = ?$
4. $720 \div 54 = ?$
5. $.5 \times 753 \times .25 = ?$
6. $15,300 \times 35 = ?$

If you want help, I'll give you a chance to divide the problems among your group members in a minute.

Problem 3

Your mission is to have your group members help you decide how to get rid of a headache. Pretend you have an awful headache, and ask them to help you get rid of it.

Who Says?

Purpose:

Teenagers will examine the purpose of the Bible.

Supplies:

You'll need Bibles, chairs, pencils, a food treat, tape, newsprint, markers, and one "And God Said…" handout (p. 126) for each group member.

Experience:

Form groups of about three, and give students each a "And God Said…" handout (p. 126). Have groups each discuss the statements on the handout and decide which ones are from the Bible.

As students discuss the statements, go around from group to group and give them hints to help them decide which statements are really from the Bible. The correct answers are in the "Biblical-Statement Answers" box below.

After groups finish their handouts, discuss which statements really are from the Bible.

Then ask:

● **Was it hard to decide which statements are from the Bible? Why or why not?** *(It was very difficult, they all sounded alike; yes, I didn't know some of that stuff was in the Bible.)*

● **What reaction did you have if you didn't know which ones to choose?** *(I was frustrated; I was embarrassed.)*

● **How is that like the way the early Christians might've felt as they tried to decide what to include in the New Testament?** *(They must've felt even more overwhelmed; they were probably frustrated too.)*

● **How did you feel when I came around and helped you?** *(Relieved; more confident of our answers.)*

● **How was that like how the early Christians might've felt, knowing the Holy Spirit was guiding them to form the Bible?** *(Good; confident; that it wasn't all on their shoulders.)*

Biblical-Statement Answers

1. Herman Melville
2. Jean Jacques Rousseau
3. Ecclesiastes 7:8
4. Hugh Black
5. Thomas Carlyle
6. Psalm 68:2a
7. Proverbs 9:17
8. Blaise Pascal
9. Matthew 10:24
10. Paul Scherer
11. Song of Songs 8:7a

Have students sit in chairs in a circle. Say: **I'm going to read some information about the Bible. Listen as I read, and every time I say something you don't already know, move one space to the right. If that space is filled by someone else, sit in the next available chair.**

Read this aloud: **It probably wasn't easy for the early Christians to decide which books God wanted in the New Testament. By that time, the Old Testament—the part of the Bible written before Jesus came—was already written and accepted by God's people.**

But deciding what should be included in the New Testament was hard. Lots of books and letters had been written by Christians in the first one hundred years after Christ. And not all of them belonged in the Bible. So in the second century after Christ, the Christians came up with four basic questions to guide them in selecting which books and letters should be included in the Bible:

1. Was the book or letter written or approved by an apostle?
2. Were its contents essentially spiritual?
3. Did the book or letter show evidence of being inspired by God?
4. Had most churches accepted it?

These questions made deciding easier. But even with God's guidance, it still took around two hundred more years to settle the issue. The Bible was finally certified as complete by a council of church leaders in A.D. 397. And it's still the same today!

After the reading, have students return to their original chairs. Say: **As we can see, there's a lot we don't know about how the Bible was formed. But God made sure the Bible came to us as he wanted it to because he has a special purpose for it. Let's look at what that purpose is.**

Form three groups. A group can be one person. Assign one of these passages to each group: Deuteronomy 31:9-13; John 20:30-31; and 2 Timothy 3:15-16.

Say: **We're going to have a contest. The winner will be the group that can tell most accurately what the purpose of the Bible is. You have five minutes to prepare your presentations.**

Let each group choose how to make the presentation. Suggest options such as a news report, a scientific announcement, a visual presentation using newsprint and markers, or a skit. After five minutes, have groups give their presentations.

Then ask:

● **Which of these Bible purposes is correct?**

Write students' responses on newsprint. All purposes the students present will likely be correct. If so, congratulate them all, and award each student a treat you know students like, such as a doughnut or candy bar. But tell students they can't eat their treats for a few minutes. Read aloud the groups' answers again, and ask:

● **So why did God give us the Bible?** *(To help us learn about him; to help us believe in Jesus; to help us find eternal life.)*

● **I gave you treats, but you haven't eaten them yet. How do you know they'll be good?** *(Because I trust you; because of the name on the wrapper.)*

● **How is believing your treat is good like believing the Bible is good?** *(God gave us the Bible, and we can trust him; if it's God's Word, it must be good.)*

Let students eat their treats.

Say: **Knowing we can trust the Bible as God's message for us makes the Bible extremely important to us. Let's do our best to read the Bible often so we can get the most out of God's message.**

And God Said...

Some of the statements below are from the Bible. Others are from people throughout history. Check mark all those you think are from the Bible.

1. "He offered a prayer so deeply devout that he seemed kneeling and praying at the bottom of the sea." ☐

2. "Do not judge, and you will never be mistaken." ☐

3. "The end of a matter is better than its beginning, and patience is better than pride." ☐

4. "The fear of God kills all other fears." ☐

5. "Blessed are the valiant that have lived in the Lord." ☐

6. "As smoke is blown away by the wind, may you blow them away." ☐

7. "Stolen water is sweet; food eaten in secret is delicious!" ☐

8. "It is the heart which experiences God, and not the reason." ☐

9. "A student is not above his teacher, nor a servant above his master." ☐

10. "We find freedom when we find God; we lose it when we lose him." ☐

11. "Many waters cannot quench love." ☐

Indexes

Scripture Index

Topical Index

Group Publishing, Inc.
Attention: Product Development
P.O. Box 481
Loveland, CO 80539
Fax: (970) 669-1994

Evaluation for *STUDENT-LED DEVOTIONS FOR YOUTH MINISTRY*

Please help Group Publishing, Inc., continue to provide innovative and useful resources for ministry. Please take a moment to fill out this evaluation and mail or fax it to us. Thanks!

● ● ●

1. As a whole, this book has been (circle one)

not very helpful   very helpful

1   2   3   4   5   6   7   8   9   10

2. The best things about this book:

3. Ways this book could be improved:

4. Things I will change because of this book:

5. Other books I'd like to see Group publish in the future:

6. Would you be interested in field-testing future Group products and giving us your feedback? If so, please fill in the information below:

Name _____

Street Address _____

City _____ State _____ Zip _____

Phone Number _____ Date _____